INTRODUCING QUALITATIVE METHODS provides a series of volumes which introduce qualitative research to the student and beginning researcher. The approach is interdisciplinary and international. A distinctive feature of these volumes is the helpful student exercises.

One stream of the series provides texts on the key methodologies used in qualitative research. The other stream contains books on qualitative research for different disciplines or occupations. Both streams cover the basic literature in a clear and accessible style, but also cover the 'cutting edge' issues in the area.

SERIES EDITOR
David Silverman (Goldsmiths College)

EDITORIAL BOARD
Michael Bloor (University of Wales, Cardiff)
Barbara Czarniawska (University of Gothenburg)
Norman Denzin (University of Illinois, Champaign)
Barry Glassner (University of Southern California)
Jaber Gubrium (University of Missouri)
Anne Murcott (South Bank University)
Jonathan Potter (Loughborough University)

TITLES IN SERIES

Qualitative Research in Sociology

An Introduction

Amir B. Marvasti

SAGE Publications

London • Thousand Oaks • New Delhi

SAGE Publications Ltd
6 Bonhill Street
London EC2A 4PU

SAGE Publications Inc.
2455 Teller Road
Thousand Oaks, California 91320

SAGE Publications India Pvt Ltd
B-42, Panchsheel Enclave
Post Box 4109
New Delhi 100 017

British Library Cataloguing in Publication data

A catalogue record for this book is available
from the British Library

ISBN 0 7619 4860 0
ISBN 0 7619 4861 9 (pbk)

Library of Congress Control Number 2003105198

Typeset by C&M Digitals (P) Ltd., Chennai, India
Printed in Great Britain by The Cromwell Press Ltd, Trowbridge, Wiltshire

Contents

Acknowledgments

This book could not have been completed without the extensive and generous support of Professor David Silverman, who patiently helped me improve this work from start to finish. I also owe much gratitude to Professor Jay Gubrium, who has both inspired and mentored me throughout my career. My thanks also go to Michael Carmichael, Zoë Elliot, and Sage staff for their assistance and consistent encouragement. Lastly, Karyn McKinney deserves my endless appreciation for helping me conceptualize and edit this work.

1

What is Qualitative Research?

Social life is full of experiences that prompt people to reexamine their surroundings. For example, an unpleasant public encounter may motivate us to try retrospectively to make sense of the event (i.e., we ask how and why things happened as they did). In many ways, all human beings are novice researchers who give meaning to, interpret, and predict their social world. This work of researching and theorizing about society encompasses an infinite number of topics. For instance, some may wonder about their personal relationships (e.g., 'Why did my significant other not return my phone call?'), while others may be preoccupied with weightier matters of social justice (e.g., 'How can we stop all the violence in the world?') or, as is often the case, we may be interested in both personal and global issues.

The specific focus of questions aside, all human beings are interested in understanding and explaining everyday experiences. This basic sense of curiosity is the foundation of *social science research*, or what may be defined loosely as the act of re-examining the social world with the goal of better understanding or explaining why or how people behave. This elementary definition emphasizes the rediscovery process that is invariably embedded in research. In a sense, the word 'research' can literally be interpreted as 'renewed search,' or 're-examination.' Naturally, most people are not inclined to invest time or effort to formally study their social environment. Social scientists, by profession, are in the business of exploring all aspects of human behavior and environment.

You may be beginning to wonder how one should go about doing social science research. That is, what criteria inform the questions we ask and where do we look for answers? Is it reasonable, for example, to conclude that an imaginary man named Joe does not return his girlfriend's phone calls because of recent changes in the lunar cycle or misalignment of certain planets? Perhaps. What is considered a reasonable course of inquiry, to a large extent, depends on the investigator's disciplinary orientation. Certainly, for an astrologer, the arrangement of the constellations would be a very useful source of information. However, to the dismay of some, astrology does not meet the conventional requirements of *scientific investigation*, which demand logically connecting certain empirical facts with an explanation of those facts. The notion that planetary movements cause human behavior leaves many logical questions unanswered. Alternatively, a more scientifically oriented discipline, such as abnormal psychology, might explain Joe's rude behavior in terms of his inability to empathize with the needs of others.

Therefore, it seems that the questions we ask about our social world and how we go about answering them depend on our disciplinary orientation. For the purpose of this book, we focus on the discipline of sociology and the qualitative methods employed by some of its practitioners. The first chapter begins with an overview of the field of sociology. We then explore the two perspectives of positivism and constructionism and their influence on social investigations. The final part of this chapter looks at some similarities and distinctions between quantitative and qualitative methods.

What is sociology?

Sociology is a social science that aims to empirically appreciate the complexity of human life. Embedded in this definition are the notions of science (strict adherence to systematic observations and logical explanations) and the complexity of everyday experience, which for sociologists, is not naturally self-evident and simple. In the broadest terms, sociology can be defined as an orientation that reveals 'the strange in the familiar' and 'places individuality in social context' (Macionis 2001: 2–5). For example, sociologists might explore why in the United States young people, who are eighteen or older, can be drafted into the military, be permitted to run for political office, and vote in elections, and yet the same individuals do not have the legal right to consume alcohol until they reach the age of twenty-one. In this case, seeing the strange in the familiar means questioning the peculiar nature of laws that trust eighteen-year-olds with guns, in defense of their country, while at the same time disallowing them from possessing or consuming a bottle of alcoholic beverage. Similarly, Durkheim's (1966) classic study of suicide is an example of how sociologists place an individual act in a social context. In particular, Durkheim's ingenious examination of suicide, a presumably psychological phenomenon, revealed that social factors, such as marital status and religious affiliation help predict the rate of suicide.

The discipline of sociology can also be defined in terms of its substantive focus. That is, sociology can be described as 'the systematic study of human society' (Macionis: 2001: 1), but this definition is problematic in two ways. First, accepting that sociologists study society does very little to define the boundaries of the discipline. Society, as a field of study, offers an infinite number of topics. It is impossible to think of anything that is not, in some form or another, part of society. Indeed, the subject matter of sociological investigations ranges from healthcare, to race and gender, to crime and deviance, and to virtually anything that involves human action or thought. Second, identifying sociology as the study of all that is social does not explain how a sociological investigation might be different from a psychological or an anthropological one. It is for these reasons that this book emphasizes the analytical and investigative orientation of sociology rather than its substantive interest. (Of course, it is inevitable that disciplinary boundaries will be occasionally crossed in this text in an attempt to better illustrate certain methodological points.)

With this general definition of sociology in mind, the next question is: How is sociology done? Asking how a particular discipline investigates its topics of interest is another way of asking about its *methodology* (a general orientation about how research is done) and *methods* (specific research techniques used to study a topic) (Silverman 2001: 4). In most introductory texts the hows of investigation are discussed separately from the organizing principles and philosophical presuppositions (theory); however, in practice, the two are intricately linked in that one informs the other. Sociological investigations make use of different research methods depending on their theoretical orientations. For example, those who argue crime is caused by 'low self-control' (Hirschi and Gottfredson 1994) are likely to use questionnaires and other survey methods that are suitable for privately probing an individual's psyche. Conversely, the view that crime is a product of societal reaction (Becker 1963) necessitates observational techniques that will allow the researcher to peer into the subtleties of the social interaction and how they transform a person's self-concept from normal to deviant.

While numerous theories inform how sociologists approach and conceptualize their topics of interest, the two orienting frameworks of positivism and constructionism have been especially influential in shaping how social research is done. The following section offers a brief introduction to these approaches and their impact on qualitative methods.

Positivism versus constructionism

For sociologists, understanding and reporting how or why people behave as they do involves analyzing and presenting reality. In practice, this means sharing with an audience a convincing account of what was observed and its meaning. You may have noticed in your readings that sometimes two researchers studying the same sociological topic may arrive at different conclusions, or offer competing reports. For example, one study of prostitution might emphasize occupational and client-management skills (Heyl 1977), while another will explain how victims of incest are more likely to become prostitutes (Pines and Silbert 1983). Which study is a true and real reflection of the topic? One way of answering this question is to use a moral compass to judge one approach as more socially responsible than the other, and therefore more accurate. The problem with using morality as an evaluation criterion is that it closes other avenues of interest. That is to say, moral positions typically don't require empirical support. In fact, a strictly moral agenda is somewhat antithetical to the idea of research, which, as defined earlier, requires a constant rethinking of what we know. As an alternative, we could bypass the dilemma of judging accuracy by replying that the two approaches reflect differing realities. If you will, they represent two truths, emerging from two theoretical perspectives, and serving different purposes. To elaborate on this point, let us explore two philosophical orientations that may have informed these studies of prostitution.

Both positivism and constructionism have to do with the nature of reality or assumptions about what is real and how it should be studied. Naturally, the average person takes reality for granted. In the everyday world, we know what is real and do not doubt its existence. This taken-for-granted view of reality is what one sociologist called the 'natural attitude' (Schutz 1967), or a way of understanding the social world that is based on common sense or what every-one intuitively knows and can agree on. It has been suggested that positivistic sociology is grounded in common sense (Filmer et al. 1973; Garfinkel 1967) or a vision of social reality that is based on self-evident truths that resemble physical laws of nature. As Hammersley and Atkinson suggest, positivistic social scientists:

1   view the methodological techniques of the physical sciences, physics in particular, as the ideal model for exploring the social world;
2   aim to uncover universal laws that provide probable causal explanations for human behavior, laws that presumably hold true across time and place; and
3   are exclusively interested in empirical observations that are described in the neutral or value-free language of science (1983: 4–5).

What are the practical implications of these assumptions for investigating the social world? In regard to the first condition, modeling social research after the natural sciences means treating the topic to be studied as something whose meaning is independent of human cognition, time, and place. For instance, in the study of prostitution, a positivistic researcher, Bill, would take for granted the common sense and widely accepted definition of prostitution (i.e., a crime in which sex is provided in exchange for material rewards). From here, he would proceed to the second condition of positivism, which is to uncover the causes of prostitution with a known probability of being right or wrong. Finally, in conducting this project, our hypothetical sociologist, Bill, would only be interested in empirical observations. That is, while he may admit to having personal feelings or judgments about the subject matter, he would take the position that, as a trained observer, who reports findings in a factual style, his research is free from bias as long as he follows certain procedures.

Nonetheless, in his attempt to predict the causes of prostitution, our colleague, Bill, may have left a number of important questions unanswered. Namely, not just why, but how does one become a prostitute? Do prostitutes believe that their actions are criminal? Are these acts indeed universally criminal, or do they vary culturally and situationally? And finally, can we really take Bill's words about being neutral at face value? Is anyone really capable of stripping their writing and thoughts of subjective biases? As discussed later in this chapter, Bill will most likely deal with these questions by fine-tuning his measurement techniques (e.g., surveys and variables) to ensure accuracy of the results, but for many sociologists, these technical solutions are not enough. They view positivistic answers to these and similar questions about how we know what we know (i.e., epistemology) as theoretically vacuous and thus have turned to the alternative philosophical school of constructionism for more analytically sound explanations.

As the name would indicate, constructionists are concerned with how human interaction helps to create social reality, or as Schwandt puts it, constructionists believe that as human beings 'we do not find or discover knowledge so much as we construct or make it' (2000: 197). Before going further into the details of constructionism, it must be noted that the concept encompasses a wide range of approaches in the discipline of sociology. In some circles, the term 'symbolic interactionism' or 'interpretivism' are used to refer to the basic tenets of constructionism, among others, 'postmodernism' may be a more familiar idiom (for a detailed discussion see Lincoln and Guba 2000; Schwandt 2000). The sometimes subtle, sometimes profound, differences between these schools of thought and the significance of their particular names are of no immediate interest here. Generally, most sociologists would agree that constructionism, as an alternative and a reaction to positivism, is predicated on the assumptions that our knowledge of social reality is: 1. subjective; 2. situationally and culturally variable; and 3. ideologically conscious. To better understand these premises, let us return to the example of prostitution.

First, investigating this topic in a constructionist framework requires sensitivity to our own, as well the research participants' subjective standpoints or perspectives. We must pay particular attention to how respondents understand and give meaning to their own experiences. At the same time, as constructionists, rather than suppressing personal feelings, we might explicitly and deliberately include them in the analysis. Within a constructionist model, subjective interpretations are not a source of bias, instead they are considered a piece of the empirical puzzle that helps us understand how people 'accomplish' social reality (Garfinkel 1967). Notice that unlike the positivistic orientation, the emphasis here is not on 'why' but on 'how' prostitution is socially constructed. To put it another way, constructionists are more interested in the work or practices that go into creating the social world and less in its causes (Gubrium and Holstein 1997a).

Second, in the example of prostitution, instead of searching for universal laws of human behavior constructionists would be more inclined to look at how the meaning and practical consequences of having sex for objects of value varies from one situation or from one culture to another. Consequently, they might ask: Should wives who use sex as a way of gaining financial leverage in a marriage be defined as prostitutes? If not, what social practices allow them not to be seen as sex workers? Similarly, constructionists might ask: Does prostitution have the same meaning in other countries? How do we explain cultures in which it is not illegal to have sex for money? Clearly, such questions guide the research project in a different direction from the search for universal and enduring causes of this behavior.

The third assumption that a constructionist researcher would consider is how taken-for-granted existing knowledge about prostitution coincides or conflicts with the research findings to promote one ideological position as opposed to another. If the researcher is a feminist, for instance, the question might be: Do the realities that are portrayed in the study help emancipate oppressed women? Or will the work have the unintended consequence of convincing the public that prostitution is a so-called victimless crime that deserves no further attention from policy makers? Subsequently, could the research results be used to advance the position that society is not responsible for the plight of needy women, who sell their bodies to survive life on the streets? The point is that the constructionist emphasis on how reality is produced lends itself to political scrutiny of all facets of the research enterprise. Such dilemmas are rarely of practical consequence for positivists, who view the social world as comprised of a set of facts that simply need to be uncovered and described in objective and neutral terms.

I chose the controversial example of prostitution to illustrate the differences between constructionism and positivism, but the distinctions are equally applicable to less sensational topics. For instance, a researcher studying the notion of 'fun' at a theme park could follow a positivistic or constructionist path. As a positivist, she could ask what factors cause people to come to a theme park? She might then proceed to ask her respondents if they suffer from a great deal of stress and if they come to the park for relief. Her analysis might lead to the conclusion that people reduce mental strain by going to amusement parks and riding a roller coaster, for example. A constructionist, by contrast, might ask what constitutes 'fun?' How do people construct the experience of being jolted up and down and side to side on a roller coaster as 'fun?'

An interesting constructionist analysis of 'fun' can be found in Beth A. Quinn's (2002) article based on interviews with 43 office workers. Quinn shows the many interpretations of the seemingly harmless behavior of ogling women. Consider how one respondent describes this ritual:

> When a group of guys goes to a bar or a nightclub and they try to be manly.... A few of us always found [it] funny [when] a woman would walk by and a guy would be like, 'I can have her.' [pause] 'Yeah, OK, we want to see it!' [laugh] (Quinn 2002: 392)

Quinn argues that by constructing this behavior as simply 'fun,' men discount other possible meanings, such as how girl watching becomes a way of socializing men into their masculine roles and how it objectifies women. Thus from a constructionist perspective, 'fun' is not an inherently meaningful social category, but its significance is derived from the social interactions in which it is used.

Having discussed the differences between positivism and constructionism, we must acknowledge that the two have much in common. In particular, both orientations are empirically grounded; they both view direct contact with the social world as a prerequisite for conducting and reporting sociological research. Unlike a philosopher who speculates about the nature of reality without necessarily setting foot outside his office, as social scientists, constructionists and positivists base their reports on systematic, empirical observations gleaned from the social world. The two perspectives are also similar in that they yield useful information, depending on the task at hand. Returning to the theme park example, if you were commissioned by a consumer watchdog group to do the study, you might consider a research design that combines positivist and constructionist concerns. This will allow, for example, for testing of the park owners' claims about stress reduction benefits, and it will generate a better understanding of what consumers want.

Finally, as Silverman (2000: 5) notes, within each analytical approach and its methodological correlates, there are variations and inconsistencies. Positivists are not unanimous on the philosophy of science, the same is true for many constructionists. The two analytical frameworks should be thought of as points of emphasis rather than diametrically opposed standpoints (Silverman 2000). The differences and similarities between positivism and constructionism are summarized in Table 1.1.

Quantitative and qualitative methods

As theoretical orientations positivism and constructionism have considerable methodological implications for sociological research. In particular, the qualitative/quantitative debate in sociology, to some degree, has its roots in the analytical distinctions discussed above. On the most basic level, *quantitative research* involves the use of methodological techniques that represent the human experience in numerical categories, sometimes referred to as statistics. Conversely, *qualitative research* provides detailed description and analysis of the quality, or the substance, of the human experience. However, there is much overlap between the two, both in practice and theory. Thus, these methodological approaches should not be viewed as diametrical opposites. As is the case with the positivistic/constructionist debate, quantitative and qualitative methods do not represent disciplinary absolutes, much less moral ones. Indeed, some researchers opt for what is referred to as 'mixed methods' (Creswell 2003), which combines qualitative and qualitative techniques.

TABLE 1.1   *Points of emphasis and commonality of positivism and constructionism*

	Positivism	Constructionism	Common themes
Theoretical stance on social reality	How can we use objective research methods to capture the essence of social reality?	How is reality socially constructed?	Importance of empirical data
Goal of research	What are the universal laws that explain the causes of human behavior?	How do situational and cultural variations shape reality?	Production of knowledge
Enduring question	How can we improve the standardized and neutral language used to report research findings?	What are the ideological and practical consequences of writing and research?	Internal variations and logical inconsistencies

The two methods are similar in at least two respects. First, they are both built on empirical or observable reality. Regardless of their methodological and theoretical differences, qualitative and quantitative researchers agree that social research should be based on the stuff of the real world: interactions, interviews, documents, or observations from, and related to, the social world that we all agree is out there. Where philosophers may contemplate the very existence of the world, sociologists, regardless of their particular theoretical position, accept that there is a reality worthy of further investigation. The second point of commonality among all sociologists is their shared conviction that the scientific study of society should have a certain logic and consistency. This means that social research, qualitative or quantitative, requires *scientific rigor*, or systematic adherence to certain rules and procedures, whatever they may be for the individual investigator. As Silverman notes: 'it is not a choice between polar opposites that faces us, but a decision about balance and intellectual breadth and rigour. Where used intelligently and appropriately, there is no reason why quantification has to be totally shunned…' (1985: 17).

The quantitative/qualitative distinction can also be criticized from a utilitarian perspective. In particular, ideological or philosophical commitment to a particular approach can be replaced with the more practical mandate of 'using what works.' From this point of view, choosing a research method is not about deciding right from wrong, or truth from falsehood; instead, the goal should be to select an approach that is suitable for the task at hand. As one researcher puts it,

> We are not faced, then, with a stark choice between words and numbers, or even between precise and imprecise data; but rather with a range from more to less precise data.… [O]ur decisions … should depend on the nature of what we are trying to describe, on the likely accuracy of our descriptions, on our purposes, and on the resources available to us; not on ideological commitment to one methodological paradigm or another. (Hammersley 1992: 163, as cited in Silverman 2000: 12)

Methods are *tools* for doing research, and one need not be committed to them anymore than is necessary to pledge one's allegiance to a screwdriver over a hammer. It follows, then, that if, for example, we are interested in comparing suicide rates for men and women, we should use numerical data. Indeed, looking at such data reveals that in the United Kingdom, for example, the rate of suicide in 1996 is over three times greater for men compared to women—11 per 100,00 for men versus three for women (Schmidtke et al. 1999: 84). Alternatively, if the question is how do men and women emotionally respond and cope with the news of a loved one committing suicide, it might be more practical to gather descriptive data that can demonstrate the quality of the experience for the grieving person. In the next section we consider differences in the design of qualitative and quantitative studies.

Differences in research design

Research design refers to the steps that researchers follow to complete their study from start to finish. These include:

- asking a research question based on a theoretical orientation
- selection of research respondents and data collection
- data analysis
- reporting the results

All social science research involves these steps, but the order in which they are followed and their interdependence varies from qualitative to quantitative studies.

One of the first steps in conducting research is the selection of participants or respondents. For quantitative researchers, the preconditions of statistical analysis require that respondents be selected randomly. The process is referred to as *sampling* and the people or objects selected from a specified population are called a *sample*. Another requirement of statistical analysis is that the sample be large and representative, the rationale being that small sample sizes increase the probability of biased results or error. In qualitative research, by contrast, who is included in the study is less about technical requirements and more about theoretical considerations. Sampling procedures in qualitative research are sometimes referred to as *purposive*, meaning that the theoretical purpose of the project, rather than a strict methodological mandate, determines the selection process. Furthermore, in some cases, such as when researching drug dealers, random sampling is simply impractical and a purposive sample may be the only option.

Another difference between quantitative and qualitative research designs is how the data is recorded. Most numerical researchers quantify their observations using a pre-coded form referred to as a *survey*. My personal experience with surveys came from a study of juvenile offenders who were charged with adult criminal offenses (Frazier et al. 1999). One of our goals was to isolate the factors that cause legal authorities to recommend a minor for adult judicial processing. Our data came from official, statistical sources as well as from lengthy court and police descriptions of the crime and the juvenile offender's background. On the official court and police reports, with the exception of demographics such as age, all the information was descriptive. To transform these documents into data suitable for statistical analysis, I was provided with a survey instrument containing nearly 1000 items. My job was to peruse endless pages of official records and code the information on the form. For example, if the minor offender had used a firearm during an offense that would be coded as '1,' a blunt weapon, such as a baseball bat, would get coded as '2,' etc. But the principal investigators and I soon realized that no matter how inclusive the survey was, many details of the case simply did not fit a pre-coded, standardized format. For instance, we might have difficulty recording a case in which the offender began beating his victim with a baseball bat and then pulled out a firearm and shot his victim. Should this case be coded as a '1' or '2?' I suppose we could have simply added more *variables* (items whose values vary from one case to another (Macionis 2001: 25)) to the survey, but the problem was that the survey was already nearly ten pages long and extremely tedious and time-consuming to fill out. To remedy this problem, we opted to supplement the form with a qualitative narrative or a storied description of the case to capture all its details and nuances. That is precisely how most qualitative researchers collect and record data. Their data is composed of detailed descriptions of the case instead of numerical codes. (It should be noted that, as discussed in Chapter 5, some branches of qualitative research, such as content analysis, quantify data that was originally collected in descriptive form.)

The third distinction between the two methods has to do with data analysis. Clearly, the dominant mode of representing research findings among quantitative sociologists is statistical analysis. This formulaic approach, which is often misunderstood by both sociologists and laymen, lays claim to an ever expanding and diverse body of procedures. Among its various forms are:

1   descriptive or univariate statistics (analyzing one variable at a time);
2   bivariate statistics (exploring the relationship between two variables); and
3   multivariate statistics (testing relationships among several variables).

Other dimensions of statistical analysis have to do with variable types (numerical or categorical) and sampling procedures used to collect the data. Needless to say that the subject matter has filled numerous scholarly volumes and has become the basis of much dreaded undergraduate and graduate courses in statistics.

Conversely, the analysis of descriptive data is less formulaic. While, as discussed throughout this book, data analysis procedures vary from one branch of qualitative research to another, there are some common themes. Specifically, qualitative researchers in general are more attentive to the role social or cultural *context* plays in all aspects of the research enterprise from forming a research question, to data collection, and to writing and reporting the findings (Bamberger 1999). Where context for quantitative researchers is treated as interference or noise (a set of intervening variables to be controlled), for qualitative researcher context is a constitutive element that shapes the meaning of what is reported.

Lastly, qualitative and quantitative methods differ in their views of the place and significance of social theory. For quantitative researchers, theory is somewhat detached from methods. (There are exceptions to this statement. For example, some advanced statistical techniques, such as multiple regression equations, are based on elaborate theoretical models.) For the most part, quantitative researchers introduce theory mainly in the initial phase of their research report to establish the rationale for the project and return to it at the end to advance the policy implications of their work. Theoretical concerns during data collection and analysis are couched in terms of statistical and measurement problems.

For instance, a quantitative study of racial discrimination would initially consider the theoretical implications of defining the issue. The operational definition of the topic would undergo extensive analytical work (Should racial discrimination be defined from the perspective of the victims, potential aggressors, or the researchers? Should it be all encompassing or focus on a few dimensions of public life?). However, once quantitative researchers agree on a definition, the measurement and analysis commence with little reflection on the definitional problems that informed the project in the initial phase. Random samples are selected, data is collected, and statistical techniques applied to show the frequency and intensity of racial discrimination according to the predetermined criteria. Toward the end of the project and in the obligatory 'call for further research,' the investigators might return to their original conceptualization of the problem to propose new hypotheses (educated guesses) or to explain why the findings did or did not support the original expectations. This process, which is sometimes referred to as the *hypothetical deductive method* (Babbie 2002: 36–38), is not typical of qualitative research.

Qualitative research tends to be more focused on the reflexive, or the give-and-take relationship, between social theory and methods. Conceptually, most qualitative researchers do not detach *how* they collect data from *what* data they collect. Returning to the example of racial discrimination, a qualitative study, not unlike a quantitative one, might begin by considering the meaning of the topic under analysis, but it would not foreclose the search for meaning by settling on a fixed definition. Instead, the attention to the fluid and interactive nature of the phenomenon would be a recurring theme in every step of the research. Indeed, for some investigators situational variation in the meaning of racial discrimination might be considered a finding in its own right. In this sense, qualitative research has the potential to be theoretically more rigorous than its numerical counterpart.

Table 1.2 summarizes the differences between quantitative and qualitative methods.

TABLE 1.2   *Comparison of qualitative and quantitative methods*

Research activity	Quantitative	Qualitative
Selection of research participants	Random sampling	Theoretical or purposive sampling
Data collection	Pre-coded surveys or other formulaic techniques	Direct, fluid, observational techniques
Data analysis	Statistical analysis aimed at highlighting universal cause and effect relationships	Analysis focused on context-specific meanings and social practices
The role of conceptual framework	Separates theory from methods	Views theory and methods as inseparable

Source: adapted from Bamberger 1999: 11–13

In the remainder of this book we focus on the vast array of qualitative methods in the field of sociology. Specifically, Chapters 2–4 introduce interviews, ethnography, and visual analysis, respectively. Chapter 5 looks at several ways in which qualitative data could be analyzed. Chapter 6 offers suggestions for writing qualitative research reports. The book ends with a chapter on research ethics.

CHAPTER SUMMARY

This chapter began with a broad consideration of the idea of research and proceeded to explain how the discipline of sociology informs research questions and the methods for investigating them. The chapter also described the two philosophical orientations of positivism and constructionism and showed how they parallel qualitative and quantitative methodologies in sociology.

One of the main goals of this chapter was to outline the theoretical foundations of the two research perspectives of qualitative and quantitive methodologies. It was suggested that quantitative sociology emphasizes technical rigor (systematic adherence to the mechanics of doing research) and qualitative sociology conceptual rigor (systematic adherence to the theory of doing research). However, it is important to keep in mind that oppositions in academic texts, not unlike the ones in everyday life, serve as useful starting points for learning the basics. As you gain more knowledge and experience about the field, it is very likely that you will move beyond simplistic dichotomies. In practice, many scholars in sociology make use of both techniques, depending on the topic of their interest and other contingencies.

At the very least, there is wisdom in knowing the opposition. Criticizing what one is not fully knowledgeable of and accepting the opposing view without careful examination is unnecessary at best and embarrassingly unlearned at worst. Extensive learning about various fields of knowledge should precede a strong commitment to them. It is usually the case that the more one learns about the opposing sides of a given issue, the more blurred the divisions become. Positivism and constructionism, as well as qualitative and quantitative perspectives, should not be thought of as philosophical or methodological opposites. Instead, they are different ways of doing research with the common goal of exploring the social world and generating knowledge. The remainder of this book provides an introductory understanding of how qualitative sociology achieves this goal through its various research techniques.

SUGGESTED READINGS

For an excellent text on the theories and methods of qualitative research in sociology see Silverman's *Qualitative Methodology & Sociology* (1985). Earl Babbie's *The Basics of Social Research* (2002) offers a general and accessible survey of the many research methods used by social scientists. For an introductory text about the discipline of sociology John Macionis's *Sociology* (2001) is a useful resource. Finally, if you are interested in the basics of sociological theory George Ritzer's *Sociological Theory* (2000) provides a comprehensive and readable introduction to all the major theories.

EXERCISE 1.1

OBJECTIVE: To apply and evaluate qualitative and quantitative methods.

DESCRIPTION: In this exercise, you are researching how gender is represented on television. While watching your favorite show, record the number of times men and women appear in advertisements, the estimated cost of what they are promoting, and the adjectives used to describe the products. Are there any differences between men and women in terms of their number of appearances? Is there a relationship between the cost of the product being promoted and the gender of its promoter?

   Now, consider the qualitative descriptions of the products. Are there any differences in the way men and women use language to describe these products? For example, which gender is more likely to make references to aesthetic features of the product, and which is more likely to refer to its durability and strength

   What conclusions can you draw based on your analysis? Comparing the numerical method with the qualitative one, in your opinion, which approach is more informative about the way gender is portrayed on television? What are the strengths and weaknesses of each?

2

Interviews

One of the most elementary forms of data collection is an *interview* which involves asking people questions and receiving answers from them. You don't have to be a sociologist to have participated in this mode of communication. As a teacher, for example, I conduct interviews with students when they want to take a scheduled exam at a later date. I ask them a few questions about why they should be excused. If the answers are satisfactory, I grant the request. Similarly, in a doctor's office, you may have to answer specific questions about your medical history. Job applicants typically undergo a face-to-face interview before they are selected for a position. Television and popular magazines entertain their audiences with celebrity interviews. In the United States, *The Jerry Springer Show* is an immensely popular television program based on interviews with ordinary people who openly speak about the most private details of their lives.

The setting and the purpose of the interview aside, the format is fairly consistent: questions are posed to individuals and they are expected to provide meaningful responses. Interview-like encounters are plentiful in everyday life as well. For example, consider how a fictitious dinner conversation between two people on a first date can take the form of an interview:

Jean: So tell me about yourself.
John: What do you want know?
Jane: You know, tell me about your interests, your hobbies, your family?
John: Well, I come from a large family... my mom and dad are divorced... .

As seen here, the interview mode of gathering information is so familiar and so widely applied that it typically goes unrecognized. The prevalence of interviews as a mode of communication in all realms of social life has led some social scientists to conclude that we live in an 'interview society' (Atkinson and Silverman 1997). From a historical standpoint, however, this seemingly natural mode of inquiry is a relative newcomer in the world of collecting data about human behavior (Gubrium and Holstein 2002).

The basic assumptions of traditional interviews

If interviewing is about asking someone questions and expecting answers, it would seem counterintuitive to suggest that it is relatively new. After all, such give and take is the basis of most conversations, and you might wonder: Haven't people held conversations since the beginning of time? Then, what is so new about interviews? While it is true that verbal communication and curiosity about the lives of others are traits that distinguish homo sapiens from most other species, interviews, particularly the structured variety, are based on assumptions that were not prevalent in earlier times. Gubrium and Holstein (2002) argue that the modern research interview is founded on three premises.

'Democratization of opinions'

First, the interview format assumes that human beings share a common experience, which any random member of society can articulate when asked to do so. Gubrium and Holstein refer to this as 'the democratization of opinions' (2002: 4). According to this perspective, social scientists use random respondents for their research because they assume every person's opinion of the world is valid and that the sum of these views paints a reasonably complete picture of social reality. Most people would agree with this position. But consider how differently you might have proceeded if you assumed only a special group of insiders were good sources for research-worthy opinions. If that were the case, collecting a large representative sample would be wasteful. (Indeed, as discussed later in this chapter, instead of large samples, some qualitative sociologists rely on *informants,* or respondents with insiders' knowledge about the topic, to conduct their research.)

Researcher-respondent duality

For Gubrium and Holstein, the second assumption of conventional interviews is the division between the two formalized roles of the researcher and the respondent. These roles and the expectations associated with them roughly correspond to a leader-follower relationship. The interviewer is the leader; he or she asks questions and in doing so decides the topic, the pace, and the relevance of what will be discussed. The respondent's or the interviewee's primary responsibility is to provide coherent, presumably truthful, answers when prompted to do so. The rhythmic give-and-take of this exchange is something that most of us are familiar with and take for granted. Thus it is easy to assume that this is a universally shared understanding. However, the interviewer-interviewee etiquette is a cultural convention that may be disobeyed in some situations, a point that became evident to me in my work with the homeless.

Over a three-year period, I spent many hours in or around a homeless shelter collecting data. Sometimes, when I approached a street person for an interview, I was given a hostile glance instead of a verbal response. On the occasions when my request was granted, it was not uncommon for the respondent to switch the roles by questioning me about my academic and social background. This role reversal, which violates the conventional interview protocol, tends to be more common among respondents who have a lesser stake in social conformity or in doing what is expected of them. The homeless and the mentally ill fall into this category.

Additionally, spending time around the shelter meant I was privy to how the homeless spoke about other researchers who frequented the area. At least in one instance, I heard a homeless person comment to another, 'I gave that guy a good interview. Didn't I?' This remark is noteworthy because it shows how the respondents knowingly play an active role in the interview process, instead of passively answering questions. While such observations have motivated some sociologists to rethink the interview protocol, for the most part, the duality between the roles of researchers and respondents remains characteristic of the conventional interview protocol.

Respondents as vessels of knowledge

The third premise of the interview format in the respondent is viewed as a 'vessel of answers' (Gubrium and Holstein 2002) or a fountain of knowledge, that could be turned on or off by the right questions. This suggests that the subjects' involvement in the interview is limited to only answering questions and that researcher's primary job is to extract answers. Let us consider the implications of this assumption. Suppose in a study of attitude toward abortion we ask, 'Do you approve or disapprove of abortion?' Presumably, there is only one correct answer to this inquiry for any given respondent, their 'actual' opinion. If the question is stated clearly, it should produce the right answer. A person could approve or disapprove. But would it matter if the respondent were a man and the interviewer a woman? Could the gender dynamics influence the substance of an answer or the process by which it is extracted? Most positivistic interviewers would concede that the context and the nature of the interaction are important considerations; however, they would treat them as conditions to be controlled or manipulated to improve the quality of the data instead of seeing them as constructing the reality or the knowledge that results from the interview. As Silverman points out,

> For positivists, an observation that interview responses might be an outcome of the interview setting would be heard as a charge against the reliability of the technique. To the extent that this possibility arises, checks and remedies are built into the research design. Similarly, for positivists, the language of the interviewee serves primarily as an instrument for the communication of social or psychological facts. (2001: 88)

As a whole, these assumptions regarding democratization of opinions, formalized roles, and respondents as vessels of answers help shape the interview process and its practice by most sociologists today. Let us now turn our attention to the different interviewing techniques that follow from, or challenge, these assumptions.

Structured interviews

The most prevalent interviewing technique among social scientists is *structured interviewing*. Named after its emphasis on rigid procedures, this approach adheres to the researcher-respondent duality discussed above. Structured interviews began to dominate the research landscape during and after World War II (Fontana and Frey 2000: 648–49). During this time, systematic studies of great numbers of soldiers demonstrated how survey-based structured interviews could provide useful information in an efficient and inexpensive manner. Concurrently, developments in the field of statistics made it possible to analyze and interpret large data sets with relative ease. Finally, the advent of polling (surveying many people on their opinion about a particular issue or a product) convinced researchers and laymen alike that structured interviews could serve political as well as commercial interests (Platt 2002: 49-51).

Early in its history in the social sciences, the term 'interview' was used to primarily refer to face-to-face encounters among respondents and researchers. The definition of interviewing has been expanded to apply to phone surveys and 'computer-mediated communications' (Mann and Stewart 2002) whereby respondents may interact with the researcher in an internet chat room, for example. Another early distinction that is of some contemporary significance is the use of the word *schedule* to refer to a researcher-administered survey instrument (i.e., the researcher asking the questions) and *questionnaire* to refer to self-administered surveys, or surveys completed by the respondent without the researchers' assistance (Platt 2002: 36).

According to Fontana and Frey (2000: 649), the fundamentals of structured interviewing include: asking the same question with no variation, pre-established response categories (i.e., closed-ended questions) and strict control of the interview protocol using a script (or a very specific description of how the dialog should proceed). Generally, structured interviewers are instructed to follow these rules:

1 Read the questions exactly as written.
2 If a respondent does not answer a question fully, use non-directive follow-up probes to elicit a better answer. Standard probes include repeating the question, prompting with 'Tell me more,' and asking such questions as 'Anything else?' and 'How do you mean that?'
3 Record answers to questions without interpretation or editing. When a question is open-ended [requires a response that does not fit a pre-coded format], this means recording the answer verbatim.
4 Maintain a professional, neutral relationship with the respondent. Do not give personal information, express opinions about the subject matter of the interview, or give feed-back that implies a judgment about the content of an answer. (Fowler 1991: 264, quoted in Singleton and Straits 2002: 70)

These instructions are based on the logic that the main sources of error, or biased results, in an interview are the methods of data collection and lack of training on the part of the interviewer. In survey or structured interviews, researchers examine how one respondent's answer differs from another, or they study 'variation in the concept being measured' (Schaeffer and Maynard 2002: 578). The variations are then linked with social characteristics, such as the respon-dent's age, gender, race or social class.

If researchers are interested in measuring how racial prejudice affects attitude toward the death penalty, or capital punishment, they would want to know how respondent A has a more or less favorable attitude toward the issue com-pared to respondent B. For example, a survey-based study found that among whites in the United States, those with racially intolerant views are more likely to support the death penalty (Barkan and Cohn 1994). In such survey inter-views, research participants' varying definitions and personal experiences with the topic (e.g., having a relative who was the victim or the offender in a death penalty case) would be of no immediate interest, unless such experiences were transformed into measurable items. Within this framework, the person asking the questions tries not to 'contaminate' the respondents' answers by getting involved in personal details or offering opinions. The goal is to ensure all respondents receive the same treatment so that variations in their answers can be attributed to differences in attitudes about the topic, and not to differences in the way they were treated by the researcher. Aside from asking questions, the interviewer should have no influence on what respondents say.

How does a survey interviewer deal with the fact that sometimes people just tell us what we want to hear? The term used in the literature to refer to this phenomenon is the *social desirability effect*. It refers to the presumed tendency among respondents to distort their 'true' feelings by answering questions in a socially acceptable manner. For example, if we were doing face-to-face interviews about how often high school students physically assault their peers, it is reasonable to assume that many respondents, perhaps with the exception of the diehard bullies, would under-report or completely deny involvement in violent behavior because of the social disapproval surrounding physical violence. Similarly, as Rosenblatt and Furlong report, some students may over-report the extent to which they are victimized due to their 'negative world view' or general dislike for school (1997: 198). For a structured interviewer, these problems are solved by rewording questions or fine-tuning measurement instruments so that they seem less obtrusive or accusatory. For example, instead of asking, 'How often do you beat on your classmates?' they might ask, 'How often do you become physically involved with your classmates out of anger?'

Survey or structured interviewers are also very methodical about the logic and tone of their questions; they make certain their measurement instruments do not confuse the respondents. For example, survey researchers avoid double-barreled questions that require speaking about two topics in response to a single question. An example of a double-barreled question would be: 'How many times have you smoked marijuana, or have you only tried cocaine?' (Berg 2001: 79). Similarly, emotionally charged or value-laden questions are avoided. It is also recommended that interviewers do not ask direct questions like 'Why?' for fear that such a direct line of inquiry could be interpreted as hostile (Berg 2001: 78). Finally special attention is given to the sequence of questions or the order in which they are asked. The goal is to establish trust and put the respondent at ease with more neutral questions before moving to the more controversial topics (2001: 81).

Babbie (2002) offers the following guidelines for constructing survey interview questions:

1 short items are best, respondents get tired of reading long ones;
2 always pretest a questionnaire, or test on a small group of respondents to catch potential problems and errors before the survey is administered to a larger sample;
3 avoid negatively stated questions, they can be confusing (e.g., 'What type of speech do you think should not be allowed in public places?'); and
4 Avoid biased questions like 'Don't you agree that President Bush's war on terrorism is a really well-planned idea?', in other words, avoid questions that begin with 'Don't you agree,' or 'Don't you disagree…'. (2002: 241–247)

The following are examples of close-ended questions from the General Social Survey (1998), a national interview survey conducted annually in the United States containing hundreds of items on a wide range of social issues.

149C. How firm are you about your opinions on race relations? Would you say you are very likely to change your opinion, somewhat likely to change, somewhat unlikely to change, or very unlikely to change?

353. People have different opinions about the amount of influence various groups have in American life and politics. Do you think that blacks have far too much influence, too much influence, about the right amount of influence, too little influence, or do they have far too little influence? (General Social Survey 1998)

You may have noted that both questions deal with the topic of race. They are meticulously worded by the staff of the National Opinion Research Center and pre-tested using small samples before they are administered to over 1000 people each year. As stated earlier, the goal of this style of interviewing is to measure variations in a concept across different respondents. In the case of the second question, for example, respondents A and B may report respectively that blacks have 'far too much' and 'too much' influence. But how meaningful is this difference? How much can we make of the fact that one person states that the black influence is 'far too much' and another says 'too much?' In this example, while the variations among the response categories can be objectively cataloged and enumerated, the meaning of the differences remains somewhat ambiguous.

To summarize, through strict adherence to technical training and procedures, structured interviews show how individual respondents answer the same set of questions differently as a function of their social characteristics (e.g., race or class) or other variables. The differences are translated into quantifiable variations of a concept and statistically analyzed. However, survey-style interviews are limited in two ways. First, in explaining the intended meaning of the findings from the respondent's viewpoint, structured interviewers would either have to speculate or simply leave some questions unanswered. Second, the emphasis on pre-coded data collection schemes sometimes comes at the cost of neglecting the depth and complexity of the research participants' experiences. For these and other reasons, some qualitative researchers prefer the less constrained format of unstructured interviews.

Unstructured interviews

As the name implies, *unstructured interviews* are less stringent about the assumptions of interviewing presented earlier in this chapter. Also referred to as open-ended interviews, they allow more fluid interaction between the researcher and the respondent. In this format, respondents are not forced to choose from a pre-designed range of answers; instead, they can elaborate on their statements and connect them with other matters of relevance. In fact, in some published manuscripts this data collection procedure is simply referred to as 'talking,' signifying its informal and conversational style. The following is an example of an open-ended interview with a nursing home resident.

Jay: Everybody has a life story. Why don't you tell me a little about your life?

Rita: Well there's not much. I worked in a telephone company as a
            telephone operator before I was married. After I got married I
            moved to New Jersey and had two boys.... (Gubrium 1993: 20)

As seen in this example, unstructured interviewers are procedural minimalists:
they simply provide a general sense of direction and allow respondents to tell
their stories.

Two variants of the unstructured format are the *in-depth* interview and *ethno-graphic* interview. It is important to note, however, that the terms 'unstructured,'
'in-depth' and 'ethnographic interviewing' are sometimes used interchangeably
in social science literature. Both in theory and in practice these orientations over-lap. Furthermore, every study could, and often does, either create its own version
of these techniques or uses them in combination. With these qualifications in
mind, the following section offers an overview of in-depth interviews.

In-depth interviews

In-depth interviewing is founded on the notion that delving into the subject's
'deeper self' produces more authentic data. Johnson (2002) lists some of the
assumptions of in-depth interviewing. First, understanding the deeper self in
this context means seeing the world from the respondent's point of view, or
gaining an empathic appreciation of the his or her world. In-depth interview-ers aim to gain access into the hidden perceptions of their subjects, or as
Johnson puts it,

> [In-depth interviewing] begins with commonsense perceptions, explanations, and under-standings of some lived cultural experience ... and aims to explore the contextual bound-aries of that experience or perception, to uncover what is usually hidden from ordinary
> view or reflection or to penetrate to more reflective understandings about the nature of
> that experience. (2002: 106)

Another assumption of in-depth interviewing is that it can and should be
mutually beneficial to the subject and the researcher. That is, in addition to
helping the subject uncover suppressed feelings through the interview process,
the researcher also gains knowledge of his or her own 'hidden or conflicting
emotions' (Johnson 2002: 106). Lastly, according to Johnson, in-depth inter-viewing provides a multi-perspective understanding of the topic. To put it
another way, by not limiting respondents to a fixed set of answers, in-depth
interviewing has the potential to reveal multiple, and sometimes conflicting,
attitudes about a given topic. Going back to the example of attitude toward the
death penalty, instead of forcing respondents to choose if they are 'for' or
'against' capital punishment, in-depth interviewers has the potential to capture
the complexity of respondents' attitudes by attending to the 'it-depends' expla-nations. In the unstructured format of in-depth interviewing, subjects can
place qualifying conditions on their responses. For example, in explaining their

attitudes toward the death penalty, the respondent might say, 'It depends on who the victim was and how I felt about him or her.'

As a whole, the procedural guidelines of in-depth interviewing encourage mutual self-disclosure in the context of an emotionally charged atmosphere where the interviewer and interviewee freely express their views about an issue (Douglas 1985). The questions are designed to go beyond the presumed surface level of respondents' feelings and into the deeper layers of their consciousness. That is to say, the inquiries are directed at the unseen or the hidden dimensions of the self. Not surprisingly, all this gives this particular brand of interviewing the quality of 'talk therapy.' Its procedures are reminiscent of Freudian psychoanalytic techniques aimed at uncovering the subconscious through free association, or random expressions of thoughts. As Holstein and Gubrium (1995) note, this mode of data collection shares with structured survey interviews the positivistic concern with locating 'truth' somewhere within the subject. The difference is where structured interviewers ensure 'truthfulness' through a stringent regime of rules and procedures, in-depth interviewers do it by gently probing the subject's presumed inner, hidden feelings. Both are relatively unconcerned about how the interactional aspects of the interview can be *constructive of* the 'truths' of the occasion, or how the interview encounter and its conditions may influence what is articulated. The type of unstructured interviewing that is more focused on the social context of data gathering is ethnographic interviewing.

Ethnographic interviews

This method of interviewing differs from the one discussed above in that it takes place in, or is related to a particular physical setting, sometimes referred to as the *field*. The ethnographic field is the social context that guides the interview in terms of what questions are asked, which people are interviewed, and how their answers are interpreted. Ethnographic researchers typically rely on informants for assistance in navigating the field. Additionally, ethnographic interviewers use observations from the field to assess the meaning and relevance of their interview data. (A more detailed discussion of all aspects of ethnographic research is offered in Chapter 3.)

Focus group interviews

In *focus groups* the researcher asks questions from a number of respondents at the same time to 'stimulate discussion and thereby understand (through further analysis) the meanings and norms which underlie those group answers' (Bloor et al. 2001: 43). According to Fontana and Frey (2000: 651, see also Bloor et al. 2001: 1–3), historically, focus groups owe much of their popularity to marketing researchers and political candidates who wanted to gauge the opinions of

TABLE 2.1 *Comparison of more and less structured approaches to focus groups*

More structured approaches	Less structured approaches
Goal: Answer researchers' questions	Goal: Understand participants' thinking
Researchers' interests are dominant	Participants' interests are dominant
Questions set the agenda for discussion	Questions guide discussion
Larger number of more specific questions	Fewer more general questions
Specific amounts of time per questions	Flexible allocation of time
Moderator directs discussion	Moderator facilitates interaction
Moderator 'refocuses' off-topic remarks	Moderator can explore new directions
Participants address the moderator	Participants talk to each other

Source: Morgan 2002: 147

their consumers or constituents about a particular product or issue. From there, focus groups gradually made headway into the social sciences and now occupy a well-respected position among the various data collection methods.

The format ranges from very structured with respondents taking turns answering each and every question to a more flexible brainstorming session where participants voice their opinions at will. Table 2.1 summarizes the differences between the structured and unstructured focus group formats.

According to Morgan (2002), the decision about selecting a structured versus an unstructured approach depends on the research agenda. For example, marketing researchers are paid to moderate focus groups for large corporations. So in order to convince their clients of the value of their services, marketing researchers have a more visible presence in the focus group interactions. They are more inclined to explicitly direct the discussion and make it more structured by refocusing tangential comments. Social science researchers, on the other hand, are not accountable to corporate executives and therefore have the discretion to allow more spontaneous group interactions. In Morgan's words: '[The] need to perform before a client who is paying the bills may be the single biggest difference between what moderators do in marketing and what they do in the social sciences' (2002: 146).

Another consideration in deciding between structured and unstructured formats, according to Morgan, is the participants' degree of familiarity and interest in the topic. It is much easier to run an unstructured focus group with respondents who are enthusiastic about the subject matter and are eager to share their views than to ask a group of uninterested consumers about the latest dishwashing detergent, for example. This implies that focus group dynamics are in part determined by the participants' level of interest. Morgan's 'ideal focus group' is one in which the moderator is minimally involved. For him, the process should start with an engaging opening question, one that is 'designed to capture the participants' interests so that they themselves would explore nearly all of the issues that a moderator might have probed' (2002: 148). As the discussion moves into areas of particular interest, through subtle gestures or comments, the moderator could encourage participants to further explore the topic.

Similarly, Bloor et al. recommend that the role of the moderator or 'facilitator' not be confused with that of a 'controller.' In their words,

> A facilitator should *facilitate* the group, not control it…. [I]f the aim is to facilitate group interaction in such a way as to understand group norms and meanings, then the … interaction [among] certain groups may be distorted by too much external control. (2001: 48–49)

However, other experts put a stronger emphasis on the role of the moderator and his or her training. Berg suggests that, 'The tasks of the moderator in a focus group are actually similar to those of the interviewer in face-to-face interviews. These tasks can be made more systematic (and somehow easier for the novice) by preparing a procedural guide in advance of conducting the actual focus group' (2001: 121). Berg recommends the following guidelines:

1 Introduction and introductory activities
2 Statement of the basic rules or guidelines for the interview
3 Short question-and-answer discussions
4 Special activities and exercises
5 Guidance for dealing with sensitive issues (2001: 121)

Regardless of the particular approach, structured or unstructured, the use of focus groups among sociologists is gaining momentum. They serve a variety of purposes. For example, if you are interested in exploring an issue that has not been studied before, you could ask several individuals to come together and share their views on the topic. From this, a set of concepts and questions can be generated for the next phase of the research. The interactional nature of focus groups can also stimulate respondents' memory of specific events and facts (Fontana and Frey 2000: 651). As a whole, as Rubin and Rubin state:

> In focus groups, the goal is to let people spark off one another, suggesting dimensions and nuances of the original problem that any one individual might not have thought of. Sometimes a totally different understanding of a problem emerges from the group discussion. (1995: 140, quoted in Berg 2001: 115)

Other advantages are that focus groups can be very stimulating to the respondents (they won't become bored), and participants have the opportunity to elaborate on each other's answers to produce richer data (Fontana and Frey 2000: 652). However, the approach is not without its problems. Some of the challenges of focus group interviewing include: 1) one person could dominate the group; 2) respondents may be reluctant to discuss sensitive topics in the presence of others, or they could distort their answers in an effort to appear socially desirable; 3) some individuals may be shy and thus require more encouragement to participate; and 4) the interviewer has to be skilled at managing the group dynamics and asking questions simultaneously (Merton et al. 1956, cited in Fontana and Frey 2000: 652).

Respondent characteristics

Interviewers are becoming more sensitive to how the respondents' characteristics influence their data collection procedures and outcomes. In Gubrium and Holstein's *Handbook of Interview Research*, several chapters are devoted to 'distinctive respondents,' such as the elderly, children, homosexuals, women, and people of color. In this section, I borrow from the handbook to list some of the issues that an interviewer should consider when working with these diverse populations.

Interviewing children

In their chapter, 'Interviewing Children and Adolescents,' Eder and Fingerson (2002) point out that there is an obvious inequality of power and status between researchers and their underage respondents. They argue that inter-viewers have to take special care not to exploit their inherent advantages when dealing with children and adolescents. One solution is to make certain that the young respondents' participation in the research is of some value to them and their communities. As the authors state:

> The researcher's desire to gain information from child participants without giving some-thing in return reflects an underlying sense of the adult researcher's privilege. However, by giving something in return for receiving information, researchers can reduce the potential for power inequality. (p. 185)

Eder and Fingerson suggest this can be done in two ways. First, the inter-view questions and procedures can be designed to help children and adoles-cents learn something about themselves or become empowered. For example, in a study of young adolescent girls, respondents reported higher levels of self-awareness and enhanced communication skills as a direct result of participating in interviews. As one subject reported,

> But since the question came up, it let me know how I felt. I think that's good. I can do this forever you know…keep on going. I'll bring a lot up with just easy questions that you would ask anybody, you know. It lets you know about yourself. (Taylor et al. 1995: 129, quoted in Eder and Fingerson 2002: 186)

Another way in which social scientists can give something back, or reciprocate, is through *action-oriented research*, or research that produces concrete positive changes in the respondents' lives and their community. For example, Eder and Fingerson note how Valenzuela's (1999) work with Mexican-American school children helped reduce tension and misunderstanding between them and their teacher.

Interviewing women

Reinhartz and Chase (2002) offer the following suggestions for interviewing women. They begin by noting that, 'Well into the 20th century, most major social science studies continued to be based primarily on men's experiences' (p. 222). The authors state that women were relatively 'invisible' in the world of social research and quote a feminist scholar who stated in 1975 that:

> Despite, or perhaps in part because of, their omni-presence, [women] remain, by and large, merely part of the scene. They are continually perceived, but rarely perceivers. They are part of the furniture of the setting through which the plot moves. Essential to the set but largely irrelevant to the action. They are simply, there. (Lofland 1975: 144–45, quoted in Reinhartz and Chase 2002: 222–23).

In large part as a result of the feminist movement, in recent years the role of women and their special circumstances as research participants has received greater attention. For example, Reinhartz and Chase write that for some women, particularly those who come from less privileged backgrounds, the interview can have a liberating effect: 'Researchers who interview women should thus understand the possibly radical impact of the interview on the woman herself. She may discover her thoughts, learn who she is, and find "her voice"' (2002: 225).

Reinhartz and Chase also suggest that for a woman interviewer, the opportunity to talk with another woman at length about an issue of mutual interest, could produce a heightened sense of self-awareness, as evident in this excerpt from Riessman's research on divorce:

> Not only did the interviewing process have an effect on them [the interviewees], it also strongly affected me. I was divorced, as my mother and grandmother had been before me, and though I was aware that this personal history had stimulated my choice of the topic, I was not entirely prepared for my response. Listening to people's painful accounts of their marriages and trying to probe sensitively for their understandings of what had happened was sometimes difficult. (1990: 225, quoted in Reinhartz and Chase 2002: 226)

Interviewing gays and lesbians

Kong et al. (2002) note that historically studies of gays and lesbians were primarily interested in how homosexual respondents were different from their heterosexual counterparts and the causes of this supposed pathology. As the authors write:

> The dominant pattern of research unfolded in two waves. In both, homosexuals were incited to speak through interviews about what made them that way and just how different they were. But in one wave, the interview was clearly the instrument of pathological diagnosis – strongly dehumanizing, rendering homosexuals sick and diseased, and often serving as a specific means for placing homosexuals in prison, under treatment, or worse. (p. 240)

However, contemporary interest in homosexuality has moved away from the disease model to a deeper understanding of the gay and lesbian lifestyles. For Kong et al., this shift in research focus coincides with two central concerns. The first is ensuring that the interview format and the written text produced from it do not perpetuate stereotypical separations between the 'normal heterosexual self' and the 'gay other.' The authors suggest this can be accomplished through creative interviewing strategies that blur 'representational distinctions' between the respondent and the researcher (p. 247).

According to Kong et al., another strategy for better understanding the gay and lesbian experience is for interviewers to openly state their interests and assumptions about the topic (p. 249). They remind us that members of the gay community are very concerned about who collects information about them and for what purpose. They cite the following field note excerpt to show how interviewers can be candid when approaching gay respondents:

> Adam [a gay research participant] produced the fax I sent him and went about asking for clarification about the nature of the research and what I meant by storytelling. I took the opportunity to speak about the book I was writing on gay men and their families, and my interest in writing about experiences of gay men we haven't heard about before. James [Adam's partner] sat and took it all in. Adam continued to ask me questions. He wanted to know about my personal background... (Mahoney 2000, quoted in Kong et al. 2002: 249)

As a general rule, we should remember that rapport is a necessary component of research involving human subjects; this is especially true when dealing with distinctive respondents, such as gays or other minorities.

Interviewing people of color

Interviewing racial minorities requires special awareness of their individual circumstances and their cultures. As in the case of women and gay and lesbians, social science research has a long history of reducing the lives of people of color to that which is not 'white' or mainstream, or as Dunbar et al. put it, 'In the contemporary context of American and Western European society, being 'white' is the unreflected-upon standard from which all other racial identities vary' (2002: 280). In practical terms, this means interviewers must take special care not to allow taken-for-granted or unquestioned assumptions devalue the depth and complexity of respondents' experiences. How is this done? Dunbar et al. (2002) offer a number of solutions.

First, they suggest interviewers adopt ethnographic interviewing techniques that take into account the social context of the respondents' answers and their experiential standpoints. Second, when dealing with controversial racial issues, interviewers should encourage their subjects, be they black or white, to 'speak out' and break the tradition of 'polite silences.' Dalia Rodriguez, one of the coauthors of the piece, gives an example of how this approach could foster mutual understanding. After viewing a documentary film based on a group of college students' open discussion of race, one of Rodriguez's undergraduate students, Karla, remarks, 'I couldn't understand why all those people of color [shown in the documentary] were so angry' (p. 280). A silence follows this question/statement. But Rogriduez breaks the silence by probing, 'Let's go back to the issue Karla brought up, the issue of anger – What about that anger? Why do you think the students of color were so angry?' This in turn produces very meaningful responses from her students. For example, a white student replies:

> They were so angry and I just didn't think it was fair. . . . Personally I think it's ridiculous that I have to apologize for being white. I can't help it that I have what I have. I have no problem recognizing my white skin privilege but I refuse to apologize to *anyone* for the position I'm in. (p. 289)

Alternatively, another white student replies:

> Well, I just don't see why people of color aren't more pissed off. I mean, really, they have every right to be. To be treated so horribly, in the past and now even, if I were them I would've done a lot more than just yelling at white students. (p. 289)

The point here is that Rodriguez recognized that silence on the part of her students did not mean indifference, and she astutely motivated them to 'speak out.' It should be noted, however, that sometimes moving into uncharted territories in this fashion without the proper rapport could be seen as offensive. Indeed, encouraging reluctant respondents to talk is a very delicate matter and should not be approached with a cavalier attitude.

Another strategy for interviewing people of color is the use of self-disclosure, or talking about one's own life as a way of putting respondents at ease. This could help gain trust and alleviate fears or suspicions about the purpose of the research, particularly, given that racial minorities' history of mistreatment in the hands of law enforcement and other agents of authority. As Dunbar, an African-American coauthor of this work about interviewing, states:

> Self-disclosure on the part of interviewers is especially important when he or she is interviewing people of color, because, like other marginalized individuals, people of color tend to regard outsiders with suspicion. Years of misrepresentation and misinterpretation have legitimated skepticism and distrust. The question most often asked of interviewers by interviewees of color is 'Who are you?' The second most frequently asked question is 'Why should I talk to you?' This is clearly understandable if the researcher has not provided interviewees with any reason they should psychologically disrobe in front of strangers. (p. 291)

Similarly, Dunbar suggests when interviewing people of color, researchers should note 'facial expressions, vernacular voice intonations, nonverbal cues, and other forms of body language' (Dunbar et al. 2002 p. 293). Attention to these subtleties helps establish rapport and prevents misunderstandings. For example, consider the way Dunbar explains how changes in an African

American respondent's voice might be misinterpreted if the interviewer is not familiar with the nuances of the culture.

> It has been my experience in interviewing African-Americans that when some respondents become excited, their voices become louder. This does not signal anger; it simply means that the interviewer has touched on a point that is especially important to them. (p. 293)

The general principle worth highlighting is that interviewers should try to understand the world from the respondents' point of view.

The active interview

As discussed throughout this chapter, the traditional model of structured interviewing and its assumptions about the researcher-subject relationship have been criticized for their lack of attention to the social context and the interactional dynamics of the interview. For many qualitative sociologists, it is evident that research participants should not be treated as mere conduits or vessels of information to be used and disposed of at the interviewers' whim. This emerging sensitivity is captured by Dunbar et al. in the following edict,

> The operating principle should be, 'Do not assume that the subject behind the respondent is merely there for the asking.' Rather, we must take the subject to have a biography that is socially and historically mediated, and proceed accordingly. (2002: 295)

For a growing number of sociologists and other social scientists the interview process is no longer limited to the simple give-and-take of asking and answering questions. While gathering information about people remains a central purpose of interviewing, exceedingly, qualitative researchers are moving beyond technical and procedural matters and into the realm of meaning, interaction, and social context.

The most notable attempt to incorporate these concerns into a unified approach is found in Holstein and Gubrium's concept of *active interviewing* (1995,1997). According to this perspective, the interview is a social occasion, or an event, in its own right whereby researchers and respondents jointly create social reality through interaction, or as Holstein and Gubrium put it, 'From this perspective, interview participants are practitioners of everyday life, constantly working to discern and communicate the recognizable and the orderly features of experience' (1997: 121). This statement implies that in the course of an interview respondents actively take on many roles. For example, a given individual can become multiple respondents when he or she prefaces answers with phrases like 'speaking as a parent' or 'speaking as a police officer.' For active interviewers, the unit of analysis, or the thing to be analyzed, is not the individual; instead they focus on how the interaction shapes the respondent's story and its expression.

The elaborate procedural guidelines of survey interviews take on a different meaning here. Instead of producing less biased, more objective data, the structured interview and its rigid rules can be seen as creating simply another version of truth, one that reflects the assumptions of the interviewer, as much as it tells us about 'real' experiences or attitudes. For example, in a study of Jewish Israelis' attitude toward abortion, Remennick and Hetsroni asked their respondents to indicate the extent to which they agree or disagree with the following statements: 'Abortions should be prohibited except for the cases when [a] woman's life is at risk,' and 'Abortions performed not for saving the mothers' life is like murder for me' (2001: 425). The responses were measured using a closed-ended survey format with five categories: 'highly agree,' 'agree,' 'neutral,' 'disagree,' and 'highly disagree.' The researchers found that '65% of Israelis were neutral or supportive of the right to elective abortion' (p. 428). This study further indicated that certain demographic variables are correlated with the attitude toward abortion. (e.g., people with below-average incomes were more likely to oppose abortion). However, from an active-interview standpoint, this survey leaves many questions unanswered. For example, does disagreeing with the above statements mean that the respondents would not personally consider abortion as a solution to an unwanted pregnancy? What we know with a fair degree of certainty is that the statements were of relevance to the researchers, that they thought people can or should be for or against the issue; and that, the respondents' attitude, given the right question and proper protocol, can be extracted from them. Whereas from a positivistic interview standpoint, the subjects' knowledge is a *thing* that can be extracted from them, Gubrium and Holstein would suggest that knowledge is relative to time and place.

Gubrium and Holstein are also critical of in-depth interviewers such as Douglas (1985), who claim that through creative and non-traditional techniques they can capture the pure essence of a respondent's emotions about a given issue. This type of interviewing does not forgo the search for a concrete, positivistic truth; instead, it locates the source of this truth deeper in the respondent's psyche. To put it another way, 'Douglas also imagines his subjects to be repositories of answers, but in this case, they are well-guarded vessels of feelings' (Holstein and Gubrium 1997: 119).

So how does one conduct an active interview? In practice, active interviewing, as presented by Holstein and Gubrium, is less about how-to technical procedures than a way of conceptualizing and analyzing the interview process. It invites a heightened awareness about how meaning and reality are created through the interactions that are embedded in the social occasion of an interview. If one were to speak of the methods of active interviewing, they might point to an apparent affinity with unstructured interviews. In a more theoretically rigorous sense, however, the distinction between active interviewing and its structured counterpart is not so much about how or what questions are asked, but the difference is more about the degree of emphasis placed on how social reality is interactionally achieved (Garfinkel 1967). The mantra of active interviewing is 'All participants in an interview are inevitably implicated in making meaning' (p. 126).

This methodical attention to meaning making has led some critics to charge that active interviewing sacrifices content for process. That its attention to *how* reality comes to be socially recognized or constructed comes at the price of ignoring the substance of what people do or say. *What* people are saying is just as important as *how* they are saying it, the critics contend. Holstein and Gubrium defend their position by placing active interviewing in a larger theoretical framework that simultaneously attends to the *hows* and *whats* of reality production (Holstein and Gubrium 2000: 97). This means taking note of the topic of the discussion as well as how and under what conditions it is articulated.

Emerging debates

Our discussion began with the traditional understanding of an interview as a research tool based on questions and answers. We gradually moved to the more analytically complex idea that an interview is a social occasion that creates a particular version of social reality. Interviewing, a once simple and seemingly innocuous data gathering method, is being critiqued and expanded into new territories. According to some commentators this is due to the influence of *postmodernism* (Fontana 2002), which for our purposes can be defined as an interdisciplinary movement that is relentlessly critical of established social conventions. Among the various questions raised by postmodernism are: How could the traditional interview model be transformed into something more liberating and empowering for the respondents? Who owns the text and the stories that emerge from an interview? Is it the researcher's story to write as he or she wishes or is it the respondents' story? (Gubrium and Holstein 2002: 16–17). These are just a few of the many concerns that postmodernists have brought to the realm of social science research.

These debates will likely continue well into the coming decades. On a more practical level, it is important to keep in mind that your choice of interview technique should be in synch with the topic of your interest and the questions you wish to answer. If you are interested in the relationship between income and grade point average among college students, a survey interview will do the job efficiently and inexpensively. If, on the other hand, you want to study how the privileges of social class shape a person's identity and worldview, you might proceed differently. For example, you might ask low and high-income people an open-ended question such as, 'What is the most important thing you want people to know about you?' and compare their answers. Or you could supplement structured interviews from a large sample with unstructured in-depth interviews from a smaller group of respondents.

CHAPTER SUMMARY

This chapter began with a discussion of the basic assumptions of interviewing. These were described as the belief in the 'democratization of opinions,' the researcher–respondent duality and the notion that research subjects are 'vessels of answers.' The second part of the chapter focused on different interview methods. Specifically, the three dominant modes of conducting interviews (structured, unstructured, and focus group interviews) were reviewed. The three styles are similar in that they all involve asking questions and receiving responses from research participants; however, there are significant variations in their theory and practice. Structured interviews follow a positivistic view of subjects as vessels of responses. They are generally based on closed-ended questions that do not allow the subject to deviate from predetermined response categories. Unstructured and in-depth interviews, on the other hand, encourage respondents to elaborate on their answers. Finally, focus groups are interviews with a number of people with the goal of stimulating discussion.

It was suggested that researchers should be sensitive to the ways in which respondents' and interviewers' attributes affect data collection. A list of respondents' characteristics and their influence on the interview protocol were discussed. These included age, gender, sexual orientation, and race. The chapter ended by considering the active interview approach and its emphasis on the interview as an occasion in which researchers and their respondents jointly assign meaning to various social experiences.

SUGGESTED READINGS

For a detailed survey of the history of interviews in the social sciences see Jeniffer Platt's chapter in Gubrium and Holstein's *Handbook of Interview Research* (Sage 2002). Those interested in the use of computers will find Mann and Stewart's chapter 'Internet Interviewing' packed with hands-on information. As a whole, *Handbook of Interview Research* offers a comprehensive and advanced discussion of all aspects of interviewing. Fontana and Frey's chapter, 'The Interview,' in Denzin and Lincoln's *Handbook of Qualitative Research* (2000) is another thorough review of the history and practice of interviewing in the social sciences. Finally, Bloor et al's (2001) *Focus Groups in Social Research* (2001) offers an excellent introduction about all aspects of focus group research.

EXERCISE 2.1

OBJECTIVES: To review basic interviewing techniques and to provide a framework for evaluating strengths and weaknesses of structured and in-depth interviews.

DESCRIPTION: This project is based on two interviews. The first will be a short structured interview. You may select a topic of your choice. For example, you might explore gender identity by looking at the extent to which men and women adhere to traditional notions of masculinity or femininity. Find a person who is willing to help you with this project and schedule an appointment for the interview (friends or relatives are usually very accommodating). Prepare a set of questions. Be sure that they are not offensive or too direct. I suggest questions like, 'Do you think it's okay for a man to cry in public? How about a woman?' Record the answers in yes-or-no format.

For the second interview, locate another subject, preferably one with social characteristics very similar to the first. Question him or her on the same topic, but this time let your respondents elaborate and take detailed notes of their comments as they speak. You may use the same questions as before but don't limit the answers to a simple yes or no. When possible, ask probing questions like, 'Could you elaborate on that a little?' Compare the findings from the two interviews. What are the advantages and disadvantages of each?

3

Ethnography

Imagine yourself on a mission, like the crew of the Starship Enterprise from the television series *Star Trek*. Your job is to 'search for signs of intelligent life.' You have landed on an undiscovered planet. The climate seems to support human life. The air and temperature are well within the tolerable limits for a human being. You seem to have landed in an area that resembles a commercial district. The structures remind you of skyscrapers and the various billboard-looking signs – although you can't read the language – provide a glimpse of what the inhabitants must look like. The displayed images show bipeds with unusually long arms and oversized heads featuring big bright eyes. It's hard to tell the sex of the inhabitants from these pictures, so you wonder if they have different sexes on this planet. It is possible, you speculate, that they procreate asexually, which would mean no male-female distinctions.

An uneasy feeling slowly creeps into your mind: Where are the people? Could it be that this civilization has become extinct? You push these negative thoughts out of your mind by guessing that it's some kind of holiday, and that everyone is in their homes with their families, or whatever their equivalent of that social institution might be. You are startled by a black shiny object, which rapidly moves closer to your position. It appears to be some sort of vehicle as it stops a short distance away from you. A being, like the ones you noticed on the billboard posters, steps off. Using the universal sign language that you were taught as a space cadet, you try to convey that your mission is peaceful and you mean no harm. Surprise! The being speaks English. Apparently, he has been monitoring satellite transmissions from earth for many years and has self-taught several earthly languages – though judging from his occasional misuse of words and phrases, his knowledge of the language is less than complete. (Incidentally, later you realize that the person you described in your travel logs as a male was in fact a female member of the species, and you wonder why you made such an assumption.)

The being introduces himself as 'Enphormant' and invites you to visit the other part of the planet, their living quarters. Since this is why you were sent there, you accept the offer, happy to initiate the mission but nervous about the unknown world you are about to experience. Minutes later, you are in the heart of the planet's living quarters. New sounds, sights, and smells excite your imagination. Your mind is cluttered with questions. As a trained space traveler, you inquire about every detail of their lives. You want to know everything, both simple and complex, about the life and culture of this planet: what they eat, how often they eat, how they raise their children, do they have problems with crime or other social ills? Your guide Enphormant appears to enjoy answering your questions. He is delighted by your interest in his people and takes pride in what he regards as the important task of representing his way of life to outsiders.

Months later your research is complete. You have compiled thousands of pages of notes and other recordings about the people you encountered. Over this time, the people of this planet have become accustomed to your presence and you are no longer surprised by their physical appearance and odd behaviors, such as snorting their food through the human equivalent of a nasal cavity. Nevertheless, the time has come for you to leave and report your findings to your superiors. You wonder how your colleagues will receive the information you have produced about Enphormant's people and culture, and for what purposes they will use this knowledge. You have just completed an *ethnography*; you have observed, participated in, and recorded a people's way of life.

What is ethnography?

In this section, I emphasize three dimensions of ethnography: involvement with and participation in the topic being studied, attention to the social context of data collection, and sensitivity to how the subjects are represented in the research text.

The word ethnography literally means to write about people or cultures, from the Greek words *ethnos* (people) and *graphei* (to write). At the heart of this type of qualitative research are two seemingly contradictory activities: participating and observing. An ethnographer simultaneously observes and is involved in the topic under study. Involvement in what one is researching could be both risky and exciting. For example, Patricia and Peter Adler studied the world of 'upper-level drug traffickers.' In this ethnography, the lives of the researchers became intertwined with the lives of their subjects.

> socialized with … members of Southwest County's dealing and smuggling community on a near-daily basis, especially during first four years of the research (before we had a child). We worked in their legitimate businesses, vacationed together, attended their weddings, and cared for their children. (Adler 1997: 59)

Naturally, the extent of one's relationship with subjects varies according to the topic of the ethnographic research and other contingencies of the *field* (the specific setting where the ethnography is conducted). For example, if you were doing an ethnography of a death row and its inmates, no one would suggest that you should commit murder in order to really understand the lives of your subjects. However, it is true that ethnographies, more than any other method of data collection, require involvement and participation in the topic under investigation.

Another dimension of ethnography is its methodical attention to the social context in which information about a culture or a people is gathered. As Tedlock puts it, 'Ethnography involves an ongoing attempt to place specific encounters, events, and understandings into a fuller, more meaningful context' (2000: 455). For ethnographers, the research findings cannot be separated from the specific location and the surroundings in which they were collected. Where a survey interviewer, for example, can deal with nameless, faceless respondents over the phone, the ethnographic subjects' behavior and responses are always linked with a particular location and become meaningful only in relation to the specific setting (with the exception of perhaps autoethnography, discussed at the end of this chapter). As Baszanger and Dodier point out, 'A study becomes ethnographic when the fieldworker is careful to connect the facts that s/he observes with the specific features of the *backdrop* against which these facts occur, which are linked to historical and cultural contingencies' (1997: 10). To put it another way, a study would not be considered ethnographic if it ignored the context and related conditions under which people's actions and statements were observed and recorded.

The third and perhaps most important feature of the ethnographic enterprise is its concern with representational issues. The ultimate product of an ethnographic research is a manuscript that describes in great detail a people's way of life for its readers. In many cases, for these readers their first encounter with the research subjects is through the ethnographic text itself. Since the readers rarely experience the described culture directly, there is great potential for misunderstanding or misuse of the research findings. To use the metaphor of a painted portrait, contemporary ethnographers are very sensitive to how their use of color and light will create a particular impression of their subject matter. Of course, many questions come up in this context. To expand on the metaphor, suppose you commission three artists to paint your portrait and each returns a different image. One seems to be a realistic, photographic portrayal, another emphasizes your idiosyncratic qualities in an abstract style, and the third returns a satirized caricature that challenges your sense of identity. In judging these works, it is difficult to answer the question: Which is the best reflection of who you really are? Ethnographic portrayals of other cultures and their people raise similar questions. For many, the answer is to balance positivistic requirements for 'true' representation with a constructionist awareness of how descriptive styles and political agendas shape ethnographic writing (see Chapter 1 for a detailed discussion of positivism and constructionism). Thus, we must acknowledge that ethnography is as much about the practice of writing as the activity of observing and participating in social life.

Taken together, these characteristics make ethnographic research a dynamic and hands-on approach that has enticed sociologists and other social scientists to enter new worlds and dutifully report back their observations to their readers. To better understand this type of research, however, it is important to consider its history, some of which is very troubling from a political and ethical standpoint. Indeed, perhaps more than any other qualitative technique, ethnography and its past have been revisited and scrutinized by critics. Let us now briefly explore some of these controversies.

The history of ethnography

In this section, I will present the history of ethnography in relation to two approaches: the Chicago School of sociology and the British social anthropology. It must be noted that to limit the discussion of the history of ethnography to the United States and England is by no means to ignore the contributions of other nations in this regard. The ethnographic approach has been used, developed and critiqued by scholars throughout the world. Admittedly, my attention to these two traditions reflects a linguistic bias: works written in English or translated into it are simply more accessible to me than let's say French, German, or Spanish ethnographies. In reality, ethnographic theories and practices do not begin and end within certain geographical boundaries. Scholars share and are influenced by ideas from their colleagues in other places. Such crossbreeding of intellectual traditions is so common that it is often difficult to determine where one school of thought begins and another ends. Thus, the discussion below is not an attempt to claim ownership but to trace the development of certain ideas over time within a familiar framework.

The Chicago School

Many sociological ethnographies are affiliated with a tradition known as the Chicago School which came into being in the U.S. at the turn of the 20th century. The proponents of the Chicago School studied the everyday aspects of social life within communities. In particular, they were interested in how ethnic minorities living in urban districts coped with numerous social problems like drug abuse, gambling, and prostitution. The Chicago School and its qualitative research agenda echoed a broader concern in North American sociology with bettering society through social engineering. Early North American sociologists combined religious, particularly Protestant, mandates for creating a better world with the language and methodology of the social sciences, or as Vidich and Lyman state, 'They substituted a language of science for the rhetoric of religion' (1985: 1).

Therefore, the first ethnographies that were inspired by the Chicago School (e.g., *The Philadelphia Negro, Street Corner Society, The Hobo*, and so on) had the very practical goals of going to where people afflicted with social problems live to meticulously record the details of the their lives and report the results to policy-makers and other concerned citizens. These publications have a common-sense, descriptive quality that has become associated with ethnographic writing. The Chicago ethnographers were somewhat opposed to theoretical abstractions. Their intended audience was ordinary people and students who presumably read their works and were moved to initiate social change. As one scholar notes, the early Chicago ethnographies 'were intended for under graduate classrooms and (unlike formal, European theorists) spurned complex, abstract theoretical language' (Deegan 2001: 14).

The Chicago School of sociology has had significant impact on the theory and practice of ethnographic research in several ways. First, it has been instrumental in presenting the urban environment as the quintessential setting for doing ethnographic research. In fact, the flagship journal of ethnographic research in sociology, the *Journal of Contemporary Ethnography*, was originally titled *Urban Life*. Second, for better or worse, the earlier Chicago studies helped establish qualitative research, and ethnographies in particular, as more descriptive than theoretical. Finally, this tradition has set the practical agenda of ethnography in terms of moral concern for the plight of the underprivileged.

It should be noted that critics of the Chicago School have charged that its preoccupation with exotic urban settings means that vulnerabilities of the poor and oppressed are displayed for the pleasure of voyeuristic readers. Critics charge that there is little evidence that the lives of the research participants are improved as a result of being studied.

The British social anthropology

Developments that began in the British social anthropology have had profound implications for all social sciences, and sociology in particular. The earliest form of ethnographic research in the British context took the form of travel logs (Tedlock 2000). Basically, those who traveled abroad provided researchers with detailed accounts of the exotic people and places they encountered. Embedded in this mode of observing the social world, was a taken-for-granted, ethnocentric (judging other people using standards of one's own culture) distinction between the familiar culture of the West and the strange culture of Non-Western countries. This is evident in the titles of some of the books based on these earlier ethnographies, such as *Questions on the Manners, Customs, Religion, Superstitions, etc. of Uncivilized and Semi-Civilized People* (Frazer 1887, as cited in Tedlock 2000: 456).

For the purpose of accuracy, researchers and travelers were encouraged to see things from the point of view of the natives, or the 'uncivilized' research subjects in this case. The approach roughly translated into a 'sympathetic method' (Tedlock 2000: 456), which involved gaining the trust of the native inhabitants to extract information. The notion of gaining trust to gather better data was also taking hold in North America, as reflected in this excerpt from a letter written by a researcher to his employer: 'My *method* must succeed. I live among the Indians, I eat their food, and sleep in their houses. ... On account of this, thank God, my notes will contain much which those of all other explorers have failed to communicate' (Cushing 1979: 136–37, from a letter originally written between 1879–84 as cited in Tedlock 2000: 456).

There was, however, one problem with courting the natives. Researchers, it was feared, could get *too* close to members of other cultures. This was a problem because the prevailing view was, and still is in some circles, that in order for ethnographers to remain objective and to accurately report their observations, they should remain emotionally detached from their subjects. So while they were expected to gain trust by sympathizing and participating in the ways of the natives, they were also expected not to take their involvement to the level of full membership. In Tedlock's words, they were 'expected to maintain a polite distance from those studied and to cultivate rapport, not friendship; compassion, not sympathy; respect, not belief; understanding, not identification; admiration, not love' (2000: 457). When these seemingly contradictory mandates were violated, the researchers were thought to risk 'going native.'

There is another, more politically conscious, explanation of why going native was a problem. As Tedlock (2000: 457) points out, ethnographers who over-identified with their subjects implicitly called into question the superiority of the Western culture and its colonial power. Going native can then be viewed as a type of 'degeneration' or the falling from grace of the presumably superior culture (p. 457). This was more than a methodological problem; rather, it meant a dangerous disruption of the political position of the observer in relation to the observed, it confounded the firmly established relationship between 'the civilized self' and the 'the savage other.'

Many of the central premises of the British ethnographic tradition are manifest in the works of the famed anthropologist Bronislaw Malinowski. His groundbreaking research especially demonstrates sensitivity to the social context of data gathering and the need to see things from the natives' point of view (Macdonald 2001: 62). Sadly, like most ethnographers of his time, Malinowski's contributions are tainted with assumptions about the superiority of the Western culture and the inferiority of the other, as is most apparent in the title of his book *The Sexual Life of Savages in North-Western Melanesia* (1929). To redress the cultural bias embedded in such ethnographic writings, some critics have called for a rethinking of the relationship between the ethnographer and his or her subjects. They suggest that the role of the researcher as someone with a particular cultural background should be made more visible in the ethnographic text.

These historical roots, be it North American, British, or otherwise, continue to influence how ethnographic research is conducted and reported today. While the traditions have been critiqued and reinvented, they remain sources of inspiration for contemporary ethnographers. The actual practice of ethnography has changed very little since the days of Malinowski and the Chicago School. Ethnography still involves observing, participating in and reporting from the field in an attempt to answer certain questions. Let us now consider some of these questions.

The basic questions of ethnographic fieldwork

In the introductory chapter to his edited book *Doing Ethnographic Research*, Grills (1998a) lists a number of questions or topics that he suggests ethnographic research is particularly suited to address. These, which have to do with perspective, relationship, social action, and identity, are briefly discussed below.

According to Grills, one of the most important topics addressed by ethnographic research is perspective, or how people see their world (1998a: 4). Unlike survey interviews or more structured data collection techniques, in an ethnographic study we can explore the 'partial, situational, selective, and often inconsistent aspects of perspective…' (1998a: 5). Ethnographers examine how people make sense of their world in their native circumstances. For example, Anderson's ethnographic research on lower-class black males in the U.S. provides a detailed account of this minority group's fears about the police and their strategies for combating potential harassment. Consider, for instance, his description of what it means to have an identification card from the insiders' perspective:

> The common identification card associates its holder with a firm, a corporation, a school, a union, or some other institution of substance and influence. Such a card, particularly from a prominent establishment, puts the police and others on notice that the youth is 'somebody,' thus creating an important distinction between a black man who can claim a connection with the wider society and one who is summarily judged as 'deviant.' Although blacks who are established in the middle class might take such cards for granted, many lower-class blacks, who continue to find it necessary to campaign for civil rights

denied them because of skin color, believe that carrying an identification card brings them better treatment than is meted out to their less fortunate brothers and sisters. (Anderson 1997: 145–46)

Anderson, who is an African-American sociologist, gained this insight from months of participant observation in the streets of a large urban setting. It would have been unlikely for him to take note of the importance of identification cards or their contextual meaning had he just conducted a set of structured interviews. It was his presence on the streets and his association with other African-Americans that enabled him to grasp the significance of this seemingly trivial object.

The second question that Grills attributes to ethnographic fieldwork is about relationships and how they are established, maintained, or terminated. As he puts it, 'To assert that human group life is relational is to attend to the various associations, collectives, partnerships, loyalties, and joint ventures that people undertake with one another' (1998a: 5). As social beings, we are the sum of our relationships. Who would we be without the various social positions we occupy in relation to others? We are sons, daughters, fathers, mothers, students, and so on. All of these involve associations with others. However, these relationships don't appear in our lives magically out of the thin air, irrespective of time and place. They are initiated, they get stronger, and are sometimes damaged over time and under certain conditions. An ethnographic approach allows investigators to observe the complexities of human relations in the specific settings that give them meaning.

The importance of observing relationships in action and in a specific context became personally evident to me a few years ago. My daughter, who was eight at the time, wanted to know more about my job as a college professor. She asked me if it was anything like the work her elementary school teachers did. I explained that it was similar in some respects and different in others. Since I suspected my answer was less than satisfactory, I took her to work with me to show her what I do as a professor. She sat in the corner of my classroom and observed me teach an introduction to sociology class to a group of twenty undergraduates. Afterward, we had a discussion about her observations. She was surprised how different my tone and demeanor was when I addressed the students compared to how I normally presented myself to her at home. Although I am sure many other questions lingered in her mind, after the visit to my class, she had a much better sense of the social context and the meaning of my profession. The professor-student relationship was something more tangible and dynamic now that she had the opportunity to personally observe it. In a similar fashion, ethnographic fieldwork provides a more meaningful and contextually sensitive understanding of human relationships.

Another topic of interest in Grill's description of ethnography is how people become engaged in various courses of social action (1998a: 6–7). The central issues here are how people get involved in one set of activities as opposed to another, how these activities are done, and what they mean to participants.

According to Grills, to untangle these questions, one must directly observe what people do:

> Quite simply, there is no adequate substitute for the direct engagement of activities and acts of the other if we wish to understand the practical accomplishment of everyday life. We cannot manufacture social worlds out of bits of text, regression equations [statistical techniques], or responses to questions that divorce the account of action from the action itself. Of course it is easier to do this, and it is less troublesome for the researcher. The result, however, is a sociology in which the people are hard to find. (1998a: 6)

It follows, then, that ethnographic research is uniquely capable of capturing the nuances of action in its relevant context. Unlike statistical procedures, content analysis of written documents (analyzing published material), or survey interviews, ethnographic techniques allow researchers to see human action as it happens and where it happens.

To illustrate this point, let us consider a well-known study of drug abuse titled 'Becoming a Marijuana User.' In this research, Becker (1993) shows how smoking marijuana depends on a range of social factors, such as having access to the drug, knowing how to use it, and getting assistance from more experienced users to assign the proper meaning to the physiological effects caused by the drug. Becker argues that for many users the sensations caused by smoking marijuana are not inherently pleasant. On the contrary, many report feeling nauseated and ill. Becoming 'high' is a matter of learning through social interaction to attribute positive meaning to an otherwise neutral or even aversive stimulus. In this case, ethnographic techniques helped Becker challenge the conventional understanding of drug use that exclusively focuses on the availability of drugs and the personal deficiencies that lead to their abuse. Becker's ethnographic approach shows the social nature of marijuana smoking.

The last question Grills raises in connection with ethnography is: How are identities shaped, maintained and shared with others? Here the issues of social context and time become especially significant. For instance, if you were to ask yourself 'Who am I?' the answer would vary a great deal depending on where you are, whom you are with, and how you feel about yourself at the time the question is asked. From this point of view, identities depend on *when* and *where*. Going back to the example of my daughter visiting my sociology class, she observed the transformation in my identity from her dad to a college professor. At home my identity as a dad means that I am affectionate and emotionally involved. On the other hand, at work, my professional commitment requires a certain degree of detachment from students. In order to avoid accusations of favoritism, I have to be neutral and relatively distanced. As Goffman (1959) notes, our identities and how we present them to others vary from one situation to another.

Time is equally important in how we see ourselves and are seen by others. For example, your self-image as a child was very different from how you view yourself at the present time, and it is very likely you will think of yourself differently as you get older. An interesting study of the effect of time on identity is Goffman's 'The Moral Career of the Mental Patient' (1993). In this research, he looks at how the identity of a mental patient undergoes changes as it moves respectively from 'pre-patient,' to 'inpatient,' to 'ex-patient.' Each stage triggers certain transformations in the mental patient's relationships with his or her significant others. For example, during the transition from the 'pre-patient' to 'inpatient,' the mental patient experiences what Goffman terms a 'betrayal funnel,' whereby he or she gradually loses trust in relatives and friends as they cooperate with psychiatric and other institutional agents to arrange hospitalization or commitment. Later during the ex-patient phase, the mental patient is faced with the challenging task of managing or hiding the stigma of mental illness. In this example, an ethnographic design enables the researcher to attend to how a mental patient's identity changes over time.

Overall, one of the central themes that emerges from Grills' conceptualization of ethnographic research is the emphasis on the dynamic nature of human behavior over time and across situations. In this context, ethnography is particularly suited for observing changes in the everyday lives of the research subjects. In the following section we turn our attention to another important question: How is ethnographic research done?

The practice of ethnographic research

The question of where to begin or how to begin an ethnographic project has many answers. Some feel that it is necessary to begin with a well-articulated research hypothesis (a testable 'hunch' about how things might be related). Others believe that the theoretical formulation should come from the data or be inductive. This school of thought is often associated with Glaser and Strauss's (1967) idea of 'grounded theory.' Still others propose that ethnographers should simply go out in the field and observe and report human behavior as they see it.

In the following discussion, I offer a practical approach to doing ethnographic research that borrows from Hammersley and Atkinson's book *Ethnography: Principles in Practice* (1983). The topics discussed below include:

1   formulating research questions;
2   choosing a research site;
3   deciding whom to observe, when and where;
4   gaining access;
5   establishing rapport;
6   choosing a field role;
7   dealing with informants;
8   recording observations; and
9   conducting ethnographic interviews.

The research question

The first logical step in conducting an ethnography is to formulate a research question. A 'good' question is important because it helps guide the research project. It tells you what to attend to and what to ignore. However, you should be aware of two potential complications. First, research questions usually change in the course of ethnographic work (Hammersley and Atkinson 1983: 33). You could start with one question and during the project restate or entirely change that question. Second, research questions are sometimes formed in the course of fieldwork. When I was studying homelessness, my work began as a general curiosity about the topic, rather than a theory or a research question. To put it simply, I was drawn to the sight of shabbily dressed men and women who wandered near my campus apartment. I started by just wanting to know their stories and gradually transformed my fascination with street people into a full-fledged ethnography of a homeless shelter.

Choosing a research site

The next part of the process is selecting a place for doing your fieldwork. For example, if you're interested in researching shopping patterns of suburbanites, an obvious choice might be a department store or a shopping mall, but keep in mind that even this obvious selection is not free of complications. For example, it can be argued that the home is a better place to study the topic because both the need and the discussions surrounding purchases are initiated there. A husband and a wife may go over their financial budget and negotiate the amount of money to be spent and where the purchase should be made in their home, long before they set foot in the mall. So the question becomes: How much does the setting tell us about the topic under study? In the example discussed here, it may be that a mall is a better place to research the effects of advertising than shopping per se.

A related point about research sites has to do with physical boundaries. Ethnographers often find that their interest about a topic may transcend the physical boundaries of their research site. For example, much of what I wanted to know about the homeless happened on the street, in parks and in the downtown entertainment district, not in the shelter itself. As Hammersley and Atkinson point out, 'Settings are not naturally occurring phenomena, they are constituted and maintained through cultural definition and strategies. Their boundaries are not fixed but shift across occasions, to one degree or another, through processes of redefinition and negotiation' (1983: 43).

So, before fully committing to a place you must case the joint so to speak. You do this in order to gain a general understanding of who the players are and how much of what you want to know takes place there. The following cautionary words about studying the gay community illustrate this point.

> The first decision that must be made by a researcher who wishes to study the gay community – unless he has unlimited time and money to spend – is *which* gay community

he wishes to study: the world of exclusive private gay clubs for businessmen and professionals? or the dope addict transvestites … or the sado-masochistic leather boys? Any extended preliminary observation will make it objectively obvious that 'the' gay community is divided – fairly loosely at the boundaries – into a hierarchy linked to some extent with status and class criteria in the 'real' world. (Warren 1972: 144, as quoted in Hammersley and Atkinson 1983: 41)

Another relevant point is 'the role of pragmatic considerations' (Hammersley and Atkinson 1983: 41). You must consider how difficult it is to enter a particular setting, what the emotional and financial costs might be, and so on. For example, as a graduate student, I was interested in researching the mentally ill. My interest was triggered by observations I made while working at a mental health facility as a psychiatric assistant (a fancy term for what my ten-year-old nephew called 'a boy nurse for lunatics'). During one of my shifts, I overheard an exchange between two clients. One man, diagnosed with schizophrenia (a very serious psychotic disorder where the patient is presumably 'out of touch with reality'), told another patient who was annoying him, 'Don't mess with me, I'm crazy.' That struck me as a very clever, if not sane, use of the stigma of mental illness. So I decided this was a topic worth investigating, but I soon realized gaining access to mental health patients and psychiatric settings for research purposes was next to impossible. So in choosing a site for your project always think through what is and is not practically possible.

Whom, where and when?

Once a setting has been chosen, another important task is deciding what people to observe, in what context, and when (Hammersley and Atkinson 1983: 46). In regard to the people being observed, one should remember that research settings are made up of participants who have diverse backgrounds and perform different tasks. The people you observe can be divided by their gender, race, social class, their particular social position, or the professional role they serve in the setting. At the homeless shelter, there were at least three perspectives that were of interest to me, corresponding to three different positions: the staff's, the clients' and the volunteers' points of view. While all three groups were part of the same shelter, they varied significantly in terms of their interests and their interpretation of the meaning and causes of homelessness. For example, the staff tended to see the homeless clients as 'mentally deficient' and lacking in basic social skills. By contrast, the clients saw the staff as intolerant and unfairly rigid. The point is there are many stories at an ethnographic site; you should make an effort to include a fair number of them in your work.

In terms of time, ethnographic research sites are very diverse. Returning to the shopping mall example, the people you find there on a Saturday night are very different from the shoppers on a Monday morning. The activities they are engaged in are diverse as well. For example, Saturday night tends to be a time for teenagers to socialize, while Monday mornings might be a time for more serious shopping, or a time for the elderly to use the mall as a walking track for much needed physical exercise. Similarly, I found the homeless shelter during the late shift was a very different place than it was during the day. The daytime clients had more immediate needs (e.g., shower, food or hygiene supplies) and they were generally sober. The nighttime clients had less urgent requests (e.g., 'Can we talk for a while?') and were more likely to be intoxicated. Also, drug activities, prostitution, and fights were more common under the cover of night. Interestingly, the physical setting itself changes in its definition over time. At the shelter, the outside bathroom during the day was used for its intended purpose. At night, however, it was transformed into a place for drug use or sexual rendezvous.

There are also settings within settings. Much in the same way that your house is divided into bedrooms, living rooms, bathrooms, an ethnographic setting is also differentiated. As Hammersley and Atkinson point out, 'Taking account of variations in *context* is as important as sampling across time and people. Within any setting, people may distinguish between a number of quite different contexts that require different kinds of behaviour' (1983: 51).

Gaining access

By now, you probably have gathered that ethnographic studies can take place in many settings. Some may be open to the public, like a shopping mall, for example. Others have more restrictions on who is admitted and who is not. Even in public places with open access, your presence and the research activity might be viewed as strange or problematic. Taking notes in a mall might seem suspicious, especially if you combine that with excessive attention to what people are doing and saying. But there is no need for despair. In qualitative research, any information pertaining to your research endeavors is considered data in its own right. In this case, the very problem of negotiating access and how your presence is viewed in the field are rich sources of data: 'Negotiating access and data collection are not, then, distinct phases of the research process. They overlap significantly. Much can be learned from the problems involved in making contact with people as well as from how they respond to the researchers' approaches' (Hammersley and Atkinson 1983: 56).

When you are thinking about gaining access, it helps to know someone who can give you access to the particular places and the information you need. Such people are sometimes referred to as 'gatekeepers' (Lofland and Lofland 1995) and their willingness to work with you could mean the difference between continuing or terminating your research. In our research about the lives of Muslim Americans and their experiences with discrimination, my coauthor, Karyn McKinney, and I had difficulty gaining access to a mosque to do interviews, mostly because of the suspicions and misunderstanding caused by the terrorist attacks against the United States on September 11, 2001. We overcame this problem with the help of an informant, or an insider, who provided us with the name of a mosque director who was supportive of our research agenda. Similarly, at the homeless shelter, I was very fortunate to have the support of the social worker, who regularly introduced me to clients and invited me to staff meetings and parties. Thus, in fieldwork, like in any other realm of life, it helps to know people in positions of influence who can open doors, so to speak, and lend legitimacy and respect to your project.

Rapport

Every relationship brings with it certain expectations about respect, boundaries, and mutual responsibilities. At work, you operate under very specific rules about how you should interact with coworkers, patrons, and superiors. At school, there is the role of the student and that of the teacher with their respective boundaries and expectations. All functional relationships are, in one form or another, built on trust, respect, and mutual obligations, or what might generally be referred to as rapport. Relationships in the field are not exempt from this rule. I suppose you could just walk up to people in the field and ask them questions; however, without some sense of rapport you could very well be ignored, or worst yet, be labeled as a social oaf who marches into places and expects people to comply with his or her demands. Given the importance of rapport, you might ask: How does one go about establishing it? It appears that there are as many variations in strategies for establishing rapport as there are individual personalities and self-presentation styles.

One way of approaching this problem is to use interest in the respondents' culture and way of life as the basis for establishing rapport. In most situations, people are flattered when someone from another culture shows an interest in learning about their ways. This is the approach that Shaffir took in his research on Hasidic Jews. He writes:

> From the outset, I determined that the most sensible explanation for my presence [at Jewish places of worship] was to claim an interest in Hasidic Jewry: Who they are and their customs and religious practices. Indeed, this claim seemed to make sense to them. Such curiosity was, to an extent, reciprocal: Why would an assimilated Jew like myself be interested in them? Nonetheless, they did not challenge me. At most, some inquired about my background and how I knew about them at all. (Shaffir 1998: 54)

Simply telling people that you are there to learn about them could be an effective way of overcoming initial anxieties. This approach would be less effective, however, in situations where there is a broader cultural context for suspicion. For example, given the intense law enforcement efforts against Islamic terrorism, Muslims would be somewhat more reluctant to accept the claim that a complete stranger wants to observe them simply because she or he is interested in their culture.

A related approach to establishing rapport is to completely assume the role of a professional researcher. This method places your interest in the context of an occupational role. Grills (1998b) adopts this strategy in his study of two 'marginal political parties' in Canada and writes in its defense that:

One advantage of establishing a clearly defined research presence in the field is that the researcher can demonstrate a commitment to his or her role.... Newcomers may be defined by some as potential police informants, members of competing organizations.... My field experiences suggests that although disproving these allegations may be difficult, adopting the membership role of professional researcher allows for some concerns to be diffused.

By professionalism, I mean to denote the process by which respondents may come to view the participant observer as a serious, committed, and relatively competent performer of the research role. We can demonstrate this to our respondents over time and through a range of strategies. A research partnership may be developed and nurtured by activities such as demonstrating a willingness to be inconvenienced to gather data, emphasizing a desire to learn, keeping confidences, and making ourselves available to respondents. (p. 86)

Professionalism could provide logical answers to many of the respondents' concerns about the ethnographer's presence among them. Questions like 'Why are you here?' or 'Don't you have a real job?' are reasonably answered by 'I am a researcher and this *is* my real job' or 'I am a student and I am doing this for a class project.'

Another way of thinking about rapport-building is that ethnographic research is ultimately as much a craft that is learned from actual social experience as it is a method of collecting data: 'As practitioners can attest, the craft of field research is largely acquired from experiences in the field rather than from formalized training in the classroom or the laboratory' (Shaffir 1998: 61). Textbook knowledge can hardly replace what you learn from direct experience in the field. Having said that, here are some commonsensical steps that might help you with establishing rapport.

To start with, pay attention to how you are dressed. Make your style of dress appropriate to the group you are investigating. It is hard to convince a group of homeless people that you respect them if you appear to be showing off your designer clothes. On the other hand, if you are doing an ethnography of a business office, showing up in jeans and a t-shirt is guaranteed to offend your hosts. If you are worried about underdressing or overdressing for the occasion, take a middle of the road approach, dress in a semi-formal style that doesn't draw too much attention one way or another. Also keep in mind that how people respond to the way you are dressed is valuable data in its own right (as stated earlier, it is safe to say that everything that happens in the field is data).

The following is an example of how people's reactions to your style of clothing reflects assumptions about social status. During my work at the homeless shelter, on the days I was dressed in jeans and a t-shirt I was sometimes confused with a homeless client by the visitors, who came there to donate food and clothes. They did not allow me to handle their donations and demanded to see someone who worked there. In contrast, when I wore slacks and a dress shirt, people assumed I was a staff member and asked me questions like what type of homeless people were served at the shelter. On the latter occasions, the donors were also very forthcoming with opinions about what should be done to help the homeless. Thus my clothing was a constructive resource, a way for people to assign meaning to my presence in the field, and it had very practical consequences for the type of data I was able to gather.

Another aspect of rapport that could be controlled by the ethnographer is the kind of language you use. Using big words and long sentences might impress some respondents, but it might make others feel uneasy. You might unintentionally give the impression that you are so intelligent that the respondents couldn't possibly have anything of value to add to your knowledge. Or they might feel that you are more interested in impressing them than in listening to them. In most cases silence is your best data-gathering tool. Once someone is willing to talk, do your best not to interrupt them. If you have to ask probing questions, make them as short as possible. (It should be noted that some experimental ethnographers approach interviewing as a dialogue between the researcher and the respondent and thus may equally share the conversation time with their research participants.)

Self-disclosure is another strategy for strengthening rapport. Telling people about yourself is a very natural way of starting friendships and gaining trust, but don't overdo it. Talking too much about oneself could get in the way. Unless you are using an innovative ethnographic technique, such as *autoethnography* (a type of ethnography that uses the experiences of the researcher as a source of data, which I will discuss in more detail at the end of this chapter), you should keep research subjects the focus of the project. Use self-disclosure if it helps bring the topic into focus or if it helps people better understand the goal of your research.

For some ethnographers self-disclosure is an ethical mandate. They feel that telling respondents about themselves both enhances their data and brings fairness and balance to fieldwork. For example, in her ethnography of a synagogue, Berger makes a deliberate and systematic effort to share her personal life with her participants. The following is an excerpt from her research:

> Rabbi Levinson smiles warmly at me, his gray beard crinkling and his dark eyes lighting up behind his glasses. 'Let me ask you a question. Do you come from a religious family?'
>
> 'Not exactly. My parents are not religious at all. But my grandparents were. They kept kosher and my grandfather walked to synagogue,' I reply. 'I think their belief is one reason I've always been drawn to try and understand faith,' I confess.
>
> He nods. 'Yes. My grandfather was a religious man as well. He is one reason why I love religion so much. You were close with your grandparents?'
>
> 'Very.' I smile with warmth of family memories. (2001: 512)

Here Berger shows how self-disclosure adds complexity to the ethnographic report while at the same time enhancing rapport.

Don't be surprised if people in the field ask you questions about yourself. When that happens not answering questions or being evasive could damage rapport. One way of preparing for such a possibility is to have a number of sensible replies ready for commonly asked questions. For example, as mentioned earlier, it is almost certain that you will be asked: 'Why are you here?' A reasonable answer is: 'I am doing research for a class project.' Being unnecessarily mysterious and evasive does not help with rapport.

The discussion about rapport so far has centered on aspects of *self-presentation* (Goffman 1959), or the process and practices through which we present ourselves and are perceived by others. For the most part, we have a good deal of control over how we present ourselves to others. For example, we can dress in a way that is appropriate for the occasion and be mindful of our personal hygiene. On the other hand, there are however, other dimensions of how we appear in the eyes of others that are not within our control to the same extent. You may think of these as ascribed characteristics, or social characteristics that we are born with. Your age, gender, race, or ethnicity, for example, are immediately noticed by others in social interactions and, depending on the culture of the setting, are viewed as important markers of your identity. These characteristics tend to open some doors and close others. In our research on Muslim Americans, my female coauthor is in a position to interview some Muslim women who are not allowed to speak to a male stranger about their personal lives. (I should point out that the practice of sheltering women from strangers and limiting their access to public spheres of life is done under very orthodox, culturally specific interpretations of Islam. Many Muslim women are fully involved in all aspects of modern life.) At the same time, we were told by one of our informants that I, as a male researcher, would have an easier time gaining access to and establishing rapport with some of the men who frequent mosques. Therefore, who you are and where you come from could be very important to people in the field. The meaning assigned to your personal attributes might constitute barriers or opportunities for your research. I don't mean to suggest that the ethnographer is completely at the mercy of the people in the field and their interpretations of him or her, but a general awareness of the culture of the setting and its expectations regarding race, gender and other social characteristics could go a long way in helping you build rapport.

Field roles

One could occupy many roles in the field. For example, if you were doing the mall project, you might assume the role of a shopper, blend in with the other shoppers, listen to their complaints and share some of your own gripes with them. Or if you work as a store clerk in a department store, you could use that opportunity to gather data. The position you assume or you are assigned to in the course of ethnographic research is referred to as *field role*. The most familiar and talked about field role is that of a stranger (Schutz 1971). This role is akin to the position of the space traveler presented at the opening of this chapter, someone who approaches another culture as an outsider with no prior knowledge. Of course, in reality, few, if any, of us will ever encounter a culture that is *completely* foreign. Even the most 'exotic' cultures are certain to contain familiar social forms like kinship structures and religious or spiritual practices. The role of the stranger is an 'ideal type' (Weber 1946), or an abstract idea rather than an actual state of existence.

In practice, there are many roles an ethnographer may be assigned to or occupy in the field. Notice that I say 'assigned to' or 'occupy' to suggest that the field role is sometimes voluntarily taken and in other cases is sort of imposed on the researcher. A formal discussion of this topic can be found in Adler and Adler's (1987) *Membership Roles in the Field*, in which they argue field roles are based on epistemological choices, structural necessities, and personal characteristics and preferences. In other words, how we fit into the field is determined by our theoretical choices, the practical conditions we encounter, as well as individual factors, such as appearance and demeanor.

The Adlers also outline three ethnographic roles, which correspond to varying degrees of involvement in the field. The first of these is what they call 'peripheral membership.' This role implies marginal involvement in what you study. For instance, if you were doing an ethnography of gang violence, as a peripheral member, you might develop friendships with a few gang members or occasionally hang out with them without becoming a full-fledged member. By contrast, the second type of field role, 'active membership,' leads to, and requires, a deeper sense of involvement. As the Adlers put it,

> Assuming an active membership role can also have far more profound *effects on the researcher's self* than are generated by peripheral membership involvement. In functioning as a member, researchers get swept up into many of the same experiences as members. While this has the distinct advantage of adding their own selves as data to the research, both as a cross-check against the accounts of others and as a deepened awareness of how members actually think and feel, it propels researchers through various changes. (p. 64)

In active membership, the researcher could experience a transformation as a result of the fieldwork. Returning to the example of gang violence, active membership would mean participating in the rituals and activities of the gang. While your original intention is to simply study the gang, with active membership, you soon find yourself getting personally affected by your new friendships and the related activities.

The third type of membership role is 'complete membership.' As the name indicates, this means total immersion into the other's culture:

> The complete membership role entails the greatest commitment on the part of the researcher. Rather than experiencing more participatory involvement, complete-member-researchers … immerse themselves fully in the group as 'natives.' They and their subjects relate to each other as status equals, dedicated to sharing in a common set of experiences, feelings, and goals. (Adler and Adler 1987: 67)

Here complete involvement is both the goal and the consequence of fieldwork. In a sense, the researcher's complete membership does not just enhance the quality of the data, but it becomes data. This would be similar to when your participation in the gang becomes so involved that for all intents and purposes writing about your personal experiences would be just as informative as writing about any member of the group.

While the concepts of partial, active, and complete membership are very useful analytically and could be helpful in describing your experiences in the field, you should not limit yourself to any one particular role from the start. Don't decide that you are going to be a 'complete' or 'partial member' in advance of entering and experiencing the field. Let the practical experience of fieldwork and its momentum guide your decisions. In practice, ethnographers often assume multiple roles in the field. That is, they could be partially, actively or completely involved in their research from one day to the next and from one setting to another.

In my research (Marvasti 2003), I struggled with finding a position at the homeless shelter that represented a happy medium between my theoretical preferences, personal characteristics, and the practical contingencies of the field. Sometimes, circumstances completely outside the field affected my data collection. For example, frequently the demands of home life and other personal relationships required that I spend less time at the shelter. On other occasions, I had to completely withdraw from the field due to financial constraints. As a whole, my data collection strategies were heavily influenced by conditions both inside and outside the field. Also, I often occupied more than one role on any given day in the field. For example, I might have begun a day with the peripheral role of just listening to the clients' conversations in the parking lot. I could then go on to the more active role of a volunteer as I worked more closely with the clients and the staff. The day could have ended with me assuming the complete participant role of the shelter's night manager. Thus the analytical distinctions among the various types of field membership roles can be blurred in practice.

Informants

In the story that started this chapter, our fictional space traveler meets an alien named 'Enphormant' who acts as his guide. My stereotypical depiction of the role of an informant (which as defined earlier is an insider who becomes the ethnographer's ally in the field) emphasized the key property of an informant: his or her expertise about the setting and access to information that is not readily available to the novice observer. In this role, the informant could:

1   answer questions you would feel foolish asking the average respondent;
2   introduce you to others who are equally knowledgeable;
3   provide access and raise your awareness about parts of the setting; and
4   help you interpret the meaning of your observations.

This way of looking at the role of an informant is not fundamentally different from what we experience when we make a friend in an unfamiliar setting. For example, your college roommate may have acted in the capacity of an informant during your first few weeks on campus, showing you around and introducing you to people and popular hangouts. In ethnographic settings, that is more or less what research informants do. However, this dimension of fieldwork also presents some ethical dilemmas. To be more specific, ethnographers are instructed to form relationships and gain their respondents' trust for the purpose of gathering 'good' data. Given the possibility that respondents could mistake our intentions and feel exploited, it is recommended that they be informed of our main purpose for being in the field, which is to research. This process is called obtaining *informed consent*. The goal is to protect the subjects against potential emotional or physical harm that could come from their participation in research (this involves elaborate procedures both verbal and written which is discussed further in Chapter 7).

The problem with the informed consent protocol is that once you are in the field for months or in some cases years, it is easy to forget both for you and your research participants that you are not there to form friendships but to do research. This problem is very closely linked to what we discussed earlier about 'going native,' but here I want to emphasize how things might seem from the informant's perspective. The informant, even though he or she has been reminded that you are a researcher, begins to see you as a friend. The emotional bonds of the friendship may very well transcend the artificial boundaries set by the terms of your informed consent. Why should this be a problem? Perhaps the following example could explain.

My first informant at the homeless shelter was a man nicknamed 'Ace' (this is a fictional name that closely resembles his real street name). He lived in the parking lot of the shelter out of his van. Since we were close in age and given my need for 'better data,' we soon began to hang out. We would go out for drinks and talk about homelessness and many other topics. During these outings, I gradually realized that Ace was well known by many people in the late-night scene, and while I had no concrete evidence of this, I strongly suspected that he supplied some of them with illegal drugs like marijuana. To the extent that it did not create any legal problems for me, I chose to ignore this suspicion and continued my association with Ace. Months later I received a call from him about 1.00 a.m. He wanted to know if he could spend the night at my student-housing apartment because he had lost his place at the shelter and apparently his van as well. In his view, he was asking a friend for help. I, on the other hand, was worried about his potential involvement with illegal drugs and the risk that posed to my conventional lifestyle. So, I turned him down and offered to pay for his hotel room for the night instead. Needless to say the rapport I had so carefully built was irreparably damaged. I did not hear from Ace after that night. I think my decision was reasonable, but I can't stop wondering if, at least in his eyes, I appeared dishonest or phony. When I told this story to a professor in my department later, she said, 'Well, qualitative research is not for the faint of heart.' I am not sure if I agree with her assessment entirely, but it is reasonable to say that because of direct and prolonged involvement with people in the field, ethnography presents unique ethical quandaries.

In the case of informants, one potential solution is to think of them as fellow travelers. This means rejecting the exploitive notion of simply using informants as sources of information in favor of a more egalitarian approach that is mutually beneficial: we learn from them and they learn from us. After my experience with Ace, I treated my subsequent informants with this goal in mind. For example, I sometimes brought a video camera to the field and helped them record their world as they saw it. We later edited the footage into short documentaries and shared them with people in the community to raise awareness about homelessness. This seemed like a good compromise between my need for data and their need for acceptance and understanding. So, much like the discussion about the emerging recognition of ethical responsibilities to interviewees (see Chapter 2), our appreciation of the role of informants has moved from treating them as simple vessels of information to seeing them as partners in a venture to gather data and to improve the quality of their lives.

Recording data

A very practical consideration when you are in the field making observations is recording the data before it fades from memory. The flood of information in the field can be overwhelming to the senses. You will see, hear, smell, touch and feel. How do you capture it all? The three obvious modes of recording data are writing field notes, audio recording on cassette tapes, and videotaping (a detailed discussion of the latter is presented in Chapter 4).

A very useful and inexpensive way of capturing what you observe in the field is to write it down. When I am in the field, I carry a pocket notebook and use a small pen to jot things down whenever I get the chance. There are two things to remember when you take notes this way. One is to jot down key phrases, concepts or generally any information that will help stimulate your memory of the events as quickly as possible and later fill in the details in the privacy of your home or office. The second point is to not be consumed by note taking to the extent of annoying those around you or ignoring other events. I make my note-taking seem like adding items to a grocery list, and while this arouses some attention at first, most people get used it after a while.

Another way of recording your observations or interviews is audio-taping. Tape recorders can be remarkably effective in capturing the nuances of con-versations such as pauses and interruptions that could escape even the most astute observers, but this technique is not without problems. First, audiotapes should not be seen as a substitute for note taking. Remember that your tape recorder does not see or take notice of the social context – you have to sup-ply that with your notes. Another common problem with recording an inter-view is that the presence of a tape recorder makes respondents self-conscious. The awareness that their words are being preserved on a medium that could be played back again and again arouses very rational fears about how the mate-rial will be used, in what context and for what audience. The informed con-sent protocol of explaining the purpose of the research is essential for addressing respondents' concerns in this regard (see Chapter 7).

In the case of one of my respondents' the fear was literally from the recording device itself. Several months into my research, I approached a homeless man for an interview late at night in the dimly-lit parking lot behind the shelter. To my astonishment, the poor man confused the tape recorder, conspicuously held in my right hand, with a gun and proceeded to raise his hands and tell me that he possessed nothing of value for me to rob. Obviously, this is an extreme and unlikely scenario, but as stated earlier, most people are reasonably concerned about 'going on the record.'

A related issue with taping field interviews is the way an audio recording device changes the content of what people say. Respondents tend to shift their speech to a more formal tone as soon as the tape recorder is turned on. It sometimes seems as if the 'on' button on the recorder activates a particular persona. Fortunately, this tendency gradually dissipates several minutes into the interview as they switch back to their 'normal' selves.

Aside from using the appropriate technique for recording information in the field, you should also be mindful of the way data analysis and collection are closely affiliated. Silverman notes that, 'in most qualitative research, unless you are analysing data more or less from day one, you will always have to play "catch-up"' (2000: 119). This general difficulty with drawing a clear distinction between data collection and data analysis in qualitative research is especially applicable to ethnographic studies. In fact, the very process of taking notes in the field becomes a sort of data analysis and theorizing in its own right, or as Emerson puts it:

> What is included or excluded ... is not determined randomly; rather, the process of looking and reporting are guided by the observer's implicit or explicit concepts that make some details more important and relevant than others. Thus, what is selected for observation and recording reflects the working theories or conceptual assumptions employed, however implicitly, by the ethnographer. To insist on a sharp polarity between description and analysis is thus misleading; description is necessarily analytic. (1988: 20)

Therefore, from an ethnographic standpoint the blurring of the boundary between data collection and analysis is a necessary component of the research. The theoretical significance of field notes is best captured by the concept of 'thick descriptions' (Geertz 1988), which according to Emerson (1988) means showing:

> in close detail the context and meanings of events and scenes that are relevant to those involved in them. This task requires the ethnographer to identify and communicate the connections between actions and events. ... In this sort of descriptive enterprise, actions are not stripped of locally relevant context and interconnectedness, but are tied together in textured and holistic accounts of social life. (pp. 24–25)

So note-taking occupies a very important place within the ethnographic approach; it simultaneously reports the observations and provides an interpretive framework for connecting them with other realities.

Your notes should bring to life your observations with enough details to help the reader understand both the meaning and the context of what takes place in the field. The following is an excerpt from my field notes about my first encounter with a homeless woman:

> I saw Terri [fictionalized name] for the first time in front of the shelter. It was a rainy day and there was no one in the parking lot except this figure of a woman standing in the rain with a yellow blanket wrapped around her shoulders. Her drenched face covered with thick prescription eyeglasses and a blue cap had a bizarre' comical quality. There was something odd about her. I suppose it didn't take a trained sociologist to realize that if a woman made no effort to get out of the rain and just stood there motionlessly, she was probably not okay. When I walked inside the building, I asked the shelter manager, 'Who's that standing out there in the rain?' She replied, 'Oh, that's Terri,' as if the name alone explained her condition.

My goal here was to use an impressionistic style to describe the people I encountered and to portray the social context in which the strange condition of homelessness had become familiar and acceptable both for the homeless themselves and for their caretakers. As Emerson would suggest, my analytical orientation influences how I write my field notes.

Ethnographic interviews

Chapter 2 presented an overview of the interview protocol and its techniques. In this section, I focus on the specific features of ethnographic interviewing. For the most part, what ethnographers do in face-to-face questioning of respondents could be described as unstructured interviewing (see Chapter 2). Broad questions are posed and subjects are given a fair amount of latitude in answering them. However, as emphasized throughout this chapter, ethnography is a site-specific data collection method, it is eternally faithful to the social context and its influence on how people express themselves. This sensitivity to the conditions of the setting makes ethnographic interviewing more than just a loosely formatted way of asking questions. In the words of Hammersley and Atkinson,

> The main difference between the way in which ethnographers and survey interviewers ask questions is not, as is sometimes suggested, that one form of interviewing is 'structured' and the other is 'unstructured'. ... The important distinction to be made is between standardized and reflexive interviewing. Ethnographers do not decide beforehand the questions they want to ask, though they may enter the interview with a list of issues to be covered. ... The interviewer must be an active listener, he or she must listen to what is being said in order to assess how it relates to the research focus and how it may reflect the circumstances of the interview. (1983: 112–13)

To be an 'active' or 'reflexive' listener means to have the ability to develop the questions as the interview, or the research in general, proceeds. This means bringing into the interview the social context, what you have heard or seen in the field.

The process is not unlike carrying a conversation with an acquaintance or a friend when you know the other person and could comfortably ask him or her very specific questions as well as broad or 'unstructured' ones. For example, during a recent interview with a Middle Eastern American with whom I have relatively good rapport, I asked, 'Thinking about your life as a whole, where do you think the immigration experience fits?' After a short reflective pause, he began telling me about his life story with astonishing detail. At one point in the discussion, he was speaking of the challenges of raising his children in his new homeland, but he neglected to mention how old they were. So, I interrupted him with a very direct question, 'How old are the children?' to which he replied 'Ten and twelve.' I was not solely interested in the age of his children but thought knowing that information would be helpful in providing a social context or a familiar anchor for his family story. Later in the interview, I shared my troubles with raising my ten-year-old daughter, which led to a sort of mingling of our stories. In this sense, ethnographic interviewing is especially based on rapport and mutual understanding. This perspective is consistent with Heyl's definition of ethnographic interviews as:

> those projects in which researchers have established respectful, on-going relationships with their interviewees, including enough rapport for there to be genuine exchange of views and enough time and openness in the interviews for the interviewees to explore purposefully the meanings they place on events in their world. (2001: 367)

Heyl's guidelines for doing ethnographic interviews emphasize building relationships and shared respect. Her specific instructions include:

1   listen well and respectfully, developing an ethical engagement with the participants at all stages of the project;
2   acquire a self-awareness of our role in the construction of meaning during the interview process;
3   be cognizant of ways in which both the ongoing relationship and the broader social context affect the participants, the interview process, and the project outcomes; and
4   recognize that dialogue is discovery and only partial knowledge will ever be attained. (p. 368)

The principles of doing ethnographic interviews, then, are not fundamentally different from the principles of doing ethnographic research in general: build rapport, be sensitive to your ethical obligations, and continuously consider how the social context influences the meaning of everything that you learn in the field.

Autoethnography and institutional ethnography

While, in one form or another, ethnographies share the methodological practices and techniques outlined above, they do vary considerably in their theoretical orientations. These variations reflect different standpoints on the source of the data and where it is collected. This section provides an overview of two prominent ethnographic approaches in sociology.

Autoethnography

Autoethnography uses the researcher's personal experiences and feelings about the topic as a source of data. This approach is based on the idea that our knowledge of the world is inevitably filtered through personal experience, or as its proponents state:

> Autoethnography is an autobiographical genre of writing and research that displays multiple layers of consciousness, connecting the personal to the cultural. Back and forth autoethnographers gaze, first through an ethnographic wide-angle lens, focusing outward on social and cultural aspects of their personal experience; then, they look inward exposing a vulnerable self … (Ellis and Bochner 2000: 739)

This suggests that autoethnographers turn participant-observation inward, they observe and write about themselves as they participate in the social world.

Autoethnographers also place special importance on 'authenticity.' For our purposes, authenticity means a sense of truth and integrity that emanates from one's commitment to emotional honesty and openness. There is a sort of moral project, a humanitarian goal that guides the practitioners of this ethnographic style. They are not just describing the world but they want to change it. They use personal experiences, be it pleasant or painful, to both inform their readers about sociological topics and to emotionally stimulate them. They want their readers to learn through feeling. As Ellis and Bochner suggest, 'When autoethnography strikes a chord in readers, it may change them, and the direction of change can't be predicted perfectly. A lot depends on the reader's subjectivity and emotions. If you want to restrict yourself to pleasurable experiences, much of autoethnography may disappoint or intimidate you' (1996: 23).

A poignant example of this type of ethnography is Ronai's 'My Mother is Mentally Retarded' (1996). This piece portrays the author's intimate relationship with her mentally disabled mother. It also shows how that relationship allowed for the author to be sexually abused at the hands of her father. Ronai uses what she calls a 'multi-perspective' or a 'layered account' to tell her story from the points of view of a victim, a detached observer and a sociologist. Her style reflects the paradoxical nature of ethnography discussed earlier in this chapter. Instead of committing herself to the role of an observer or a full participant through her text, she fluidly moves between these roles and takes the reader along on an intense psychological journey. Here is a taste of how her work feels and sounds:

> My father, Frank Gross (no lie, pronounced 'Grass') Rambo, had a police record as a child molester, a rapist, and an exhibitionist. He was also violent. Even though we were on public assistance, our lives were much calmer during the time he was in prison. Her beating

me [referring to her mother] was an enormous betrayal. Yes, I needed to be disciplined, but this was not a spanking. This was the kind of beating Frank dished out. (1996: 121)

As an autoethnographer, Ronai does not shy away from revealing the personal. On the contrary, she makes the personal both the site and the source of her data.

Institutional ethnography

Where autoethnography can be loosely described as the ethnography of the self, institutional ethnography is about the 'big picture.' It is the detailed description and analysis of how larger social organizations operate. Inspired by the works of Smith (1996), DeVault and McCoy (2002) write that institutional ethnography aims to understand 'relations of ruling,' or how social power is practiced and implemented to shape human activities in organizational settings:

> Institutional ethnography takes for its entry point the experiences of specific individuals whose everyday activities are in some way hooked into, shaped by, and constituent of institutional relations under exploration. The term ethnography highlights the importance of research methods that can discover and explore these everyday activities and their positioning within extended sequences of action. (p. 753)

This ethnographic perspective aims to understand how individual actors fit within a larger framework of institutional practices. For example, an institutional ethnographer could study how universities construct different types of students through their grading practices. I personally find it remarkable that students readily accept a grading system that distinguishes an 'A' from a 'B' based on a margin that could be as small as a half a point on a grading scale. As an institutional ethnographer, you would ask: What social conditions make it possible for university faculty to practice this kind of authority over their students? (Of course, I am not suggesting you should badger your instructors about the unfairness of their exams.)

Gubrium's book *Out of Control* (1992) is a good example of an institutional ethnography of two family therapy facilities. This work shows with remarkable analytical clarity how competing notions of 'family disorder' are crafted by the staff and their clients in two counseling centers. In Gubrium's words:

> This book is about domestic disorder. … It examines how human service professionals, clients, kin, and significant others in two treatment programs with different images of the home construe domestic disorder in family therapy and thereby come to understand troubles. (p. 5)

Gubrium's ethnography demonstrates how one institution attributes family disorder to lack of authority and the other highlights insufficient emotional openness as the source of the problem. The task of the institutional ethnographer here is to show through careful observations how the varying policies and interactions at the two sites lead to two relatively opposite interpretations of the same problem.

In terms of its procedures, institutional ethnography relies on the same general principles that ethnographers in general use. Interviews, participant-observation and personal experience could all be incorporated into this type of research. As stated earlier, the variations in the practice of ethnography are not as much about methods as they are about differing theoretical positions on the topic under study and the sources and sites of data (see Chapter 5 for a more in-depth discussion on the relationship between theory and methods).

CHAPTER SUMMARY

This chapter began with a general description of the term 'ethnography' as studying and writing about another culture. The history of ethnography was then discussed in relation to the Chicago School of urban sociology and the British tradition of social anthropology. I suggested that the field has become much more theoretically self-conscious. In particular, more attention is now given to ethnography's association with a colonial past. Furthermore, assumptions about 'going native' and the relationship between the fieldworker and his or her subjects have been critiqued and reinvented. I also presented the basic themes of the ethnographic research (i.e., perspective, relationship, and identities).

The practice of ethnography followed next. The core ideas here were respectively: gaining entry, establishing rapport, field roles, the role of informants, recording data, and conducting interviews. It was argued that the theory and practice of ethnographic research are inseparable, each methodological step accompanies certain analytical choices. I suggested that the overall theme of ethnography can be described as connecting observations with a particular social context and a set of relationships. The chapter ended by discussing two types of ethnographic research: autoethnography and institutional ethnography. The former views the researcher's self as the source of data as well as the site of data collection, whereas the latter focuses on 'relations of ruling' or how social institutions through their policies and practices shape human activities and identities.

SUGGESTED READINGS

For a brief but comprehensive discussion of the history of ethnography and its various genres see Barbara Tedlock's chapter 'Ethnography and Ethnographic Representation' in Denzin and Lincoln's *Handbook of Qualitative Research* (2000). A more detailed discussion of all aspect of ethnography can be found in Atkinson, Coffey, Delamont, Lofland, and Lofland's *Handbook of Ethnography* (2000). Hammersley and Atkinson's *Ethnography: Principles in Practice* (1983) is an excellent resource for those who are interested in designing an ethnographic project from start to the finish.

EXERCISE 3.1

OBJECTIVE: To conduct an ethnographic study of how heterosexual relationships are performed in public places using the methods discussed in this chapter.

DESCRIPTION: Visit the food court at a local shopping mall, preferably on a weekend when it is crowded and you are less likely to be noticed. You can record your notes on a napkin, or if you prefer bring a pocket notebook to write on. Pay attention to how gender roles are enacted by couples. Who orders the food? Who selects where to sit? Who puts away the trash after the couple is done eating? Do they share their food? If so, which gender usually makes the first offering? Or does one gender or the other simply begin to sample from the other's plate without invitation? Does this cause any conflict, or does it seem to be part of the way the couple has learned to interact? Record your answers to these questions and other items of relevance you observe at this setting. Organize your notes into a short paper that includes the major components of an ethnography as discussed in this chapter (e.g., access, rapport and field role).

4

Visual Sociology

A group of tourists take pictures of the Eiffel Tower, family members gather around a Christmas tree to 'capture the moment,' a photo journalist in a war zone frantically points his camera at the horrors of war. What do these examples have in common? They all involve documenting moments in the flow of social life. Still photos, videos, cinematic images and television programs are ways through which we are regularly exposed to the visual in our daily lives. Furthermore, lower costs and more accessible technology have made it possible for many of us to create images of our own surroundings. We are no longer just consumers but also producers of visual media. In a matter of a several decades, the visual has become much more widely used and available than the text. To the chagrin of academics, most people spend more hours watching 'the tube' than reading printed media. For example, when a friend recommends a good book, we might respond with, 'I'll wait till the movie comes out.'

What is the impact of this trend on the qualitative study of social life? This chapter explores this question from several angles. I begin by considering the place of the visual in the broader cultural contexts of our time (i.e., 'What does it mean to be visually oriented?'). I then offer an overview of the history of visual work in the discipline of sociology. The next topic of interest is how 'pictorial and filmic materials' (a phrase borrowed from Ball and Smith 2001: 302) are used by social scientists. After this discussion, the chapter offers specific how-to, technical advice on the analysis and production of visual data.

The visual culture

This section briefly discusses the place of the visual in Western societies. Let us begin by thinking about the different pictorial and filmic images we come across in an average day. If you are like me, you start your day with the latest news on television (local and international news, the weather report, and so on). Or perhaps you read the newspaper and there on the front page, you find a photo that grabs your attention. On the way to work or school, there are advertisements everywhere, typically portraying young attractive people consuming products that supposedly we all want and cannot do without. Of course, for most of us, getting home at the end of the day is synonymous with sitting in front of the television set and watching our favorite programs. It may not occur to you at first glance that what you watch throughout the day forms an essential part of your knowledge about your social world.

Many years ago, my college roommate insisted that we did not have a TV in our apartment because he thought it would interfere with our studies. Reluctantly, I went along. Toward the end of this six-month no-TV regimen, it was glaringly clear that I was out of touch with the cultural tempo of my society. Not watching TV meant that I was culturally illiterate. For example, during this period, there was a famous commercial that had worked its way into the everyday vernacular. It showed a frail woman in her seventies at a fast food restaurant. Annoyed with the small size of her hamburger meat, she yells at the workers, 'WHERE'S THE BEEF?' The question had gradually become a hip way of asking about the substance of an argument. Ignorant of all this, during a class discussion about social inequality in the U.S., I was dumbfounded when a classmate interrupted me with the question, 'Where's the beef?' 'At a grocery store, I presume.' I responded matter-of-factly. Everyone laughed. Of course, I had no idea what any of this meant. The point is that a general awareness of the visual aspects of one's culture has become an essential criterion for full membership in modern societies.

This tendency is what some researchers have labeled 'visual culture' (Evans and Hall 1999; Rose 2001). The phrase 'visual culture' brings up two questions: 1. what is 'visual?' and 2. what is 'culture?' Regarding the first question, the word 'visual' for our purposes refers to pictures, video, film, TV programs and ads. The answer to the second question is more difficult since the concept of culture has been defined in many different ways by sociologists. For example, some define culture as a shared way of life and others may regard it as the everyday practices that help us interact with others and make sense of our social world. We will not settle this question here. Suffice it to say that the latter interpretation (i.e. culture as a set of practices and ways of understanding) is more likely to make its way into the discussions in this chapter.

With these rudimentary concepts in mind, we might ask: What are the implications of a 'visual culture?' An excellent discussion of this topic is offered in Rose's *Visual Methodologies* (2001), where she argues that the notion of a visual culture implies that:

1   Visual imagery is a powerful medium worthy of investigation.
2   The visual image is constructive of reality rather than simply being descriptive of it.
3   Visual images offer particular ways of seeing social issues.
4   The visual is embedded in a wider cultural context.
5   The influence of the image is at least in part dependent on its audience: different people view and understand images differently.

Let us examine each of these premises. According to Rose, that we belong to and participate in a visual culture means the status of the visual has reached, if not surpassed, that of the written word. Many of your textbooks may use photos as a way of illustrating the text or 'jazzing up' an otherwise boring discussion. However, from the perspective of a visual culture, the pictures are just as important as the words that surround them. To put it another way, the illustrations tell their own stories. For example, consider the magazine cover photos you see at a newsstand. How often do you construct a story just from looking at the picture? A picture of a female model on a fashion magazine, let's say. You don't have to do much reading to know you are looking at a cultural symbol of beauty whose attributes are to be desired. Notice that the cover doesn't tell you about her intelligence or her professional accomplishments, but that she is exceptionally beautiful. Presumably, the model's attractiveness is inherently good, for her as a woman, for the men who lust after her, and for other women who should want to be like her. That is the story. Indeed, such images are designed with the explicit intent of making words seem redundant. This may seem like an obtuse way of making the simple argument that 'a picture is worth a thousand words,' but the point is somewhat more profound than that. The notion of the visual culture means that the picture *is* a thousand words. It doesn't have to compete with the words. In Rose's words, 'visual images can be powerful and seductive in their own right' (2001: 10).

Rose's second assumption regarding visual culture is that images, still or moving, are constructive of reality, they create what we see as much as they are 'realistic' representations of it. Picture a war zone, for example. On one side a group of women mourning the loss of their children after a recent aerial bombing. The women are hysterical. They have to be held back by the crowd as they lunge forward, straining to throw their bodies atop their dead loved ones. Farther ahead, a mob of menacing-looking men is shouting slogans. They fire their machine guns into the air with one hand and raise a clenched fist with the other. You are the photojournalist reporting this event for an international newspaper. Which sight makes a better picture, that of grieving women or the rabid men? Perhaps you decide to shoot both. But what if your editor decided there was only room for one of the two on the front page? Your decision could mean the difference between 'constructing' your subjects as victims or potential aggressors. In this way, your visual work both creates and describes the reality of what you observe.

The third aspect of visual culture, according to Rose, is that images provide us with ways of seeing a particular issue. Returning to the example of a cover girl, the picture doesn't point to potential weight problems or the fact that the model might be malnutritioned. What we see, given the lighting, the clothing, and the makeup used in the setting, is physical attractiveness. Also note that in such photos the women are not involved in any activities (they are not doing anything). They simply stand there as objects to be admired, things of physical beauty.

Another example of how the visual dictates a way of seeing can be found in sports car commercials that typically target young men. What you see in the TV advertisement is a young man who, after driving a certain car, becomes more exciting, more attractive to the opposite sex, more virile. In one ad run on American TV, two women are shown fighting over a man's attention at a dinner party after they notice he drives an expensive car. In this commercial the driver is never shown. His physical appearance is irrelevant, it is his car that defines his presence for the audience and the women in the commercial. Thus the visual, in this case a shiny sports car, does not just provide *what* we see, but it also gives us a context for seeing. Regarding the car, it is not just a means of transportation, but it becomes visually defined as an object that magically transforms a dull person into a sexy adventurer.

Rose's fourth point is reflected in the phrase 'visual culture' itself. The ways of seeing the visual described above are culturally bound. When we see a picture, we view it using our knowledge about social relations and meanings in our culture. The picture of a model on a magazine cover receives its meaning from the structure of male-female relations in Western societies. That a woman's body can be viewed as an object tells us a good deal about her place in society in relation to men. Look at your own family photos. For example, what is the place of your father in relation to the rest of the family? Is he usually in the center of the photographs, surrounded by the other members of the family? If that is the case, what cultural value can be deduced from this observation?

Even the way we pose for pictures is very telling about our cultural conventions. I am sometimes irritated by the one-two-three-say-cheese routine. It seems disingenuous to fake a smile by saying a word that forces your mouth into position. But from a cultural standpoint, smiling at the camera is a required friendly gesture. It tells the would-be viewer that you didn't mind being photographed and that you are pleased to share your likeness with them. On the other hand, a stern look could mean you are taking the whole thing too seriously. In the case of my eighty-year-old father and his generation, photography was a serious business almost exclusively used for official purposes. Therefore, to this day, he insists on having his finest suit on for a photo shoot, when he gets in front of the camera, he stands fully erect, shoulders and chin up, without a smile. My father's behavior reflects his cultural interpretation of the occasion of having a picture taken.

In the above example, we should also consider how material culture or technology plays a part in the way we pose for pictures. Early photography was slow. It took several minutes for things to be recorded on the film during which time the subject had to stay motionless in front of the camera or else the picture would come out blurred (Chaplin 1994: 204). So people like my father were trained to be stiff when they had their photos taken. Looking at the old photos of your grandparents, you may have noticed that they also appear rigid or even uncomfortable in front of the camera. What I am suggesting here is that the production and meaning of visual materials are never without a cultural context.

Rose's last point concerning a visual culture is that it matters a great deal which audience is viewing the image. Men might look at a photo of a female fashion model with lust, whereas for women the focal point could be the model's choice of shoes or other attire. In the example of a photo from a war zone, the person sympathetic to their cause would view the shouting men with their machine guns as resistance fighters. By contrast, to the eyes of another viewer they might seem like dangerous zealots. The visual and its creators are not sole arbiters of how an image is perceived. Instead, the visual product is interpreted in different ways depending on the audience and its cultural sensibilities.

My students often recommend, or even demand, that I see a particular movie because they feel that it is a good illustration of an issue we discussed in class. Occasionally, I follow their recommendations, but many times I sadly report back that I saw the movie and just didn't get it. In this case, the widening intergenerational gap between my students and me means that we see the same visual piece very differently. I see gratuitous violence and they see a poignant social commentary on the human condition. According to Rose, then, we cannot dismiss the capacity of the audience to view the visual in novel and unexpected ways.

In summary, Rose alerts us to the significance of a growing visual culture with its own sensibilities. She explains how the visual can be much more than a method of illustrating the written text. With this general appreciation for the visual and its accompanying analytical insights, let us now probe the history of the visual in the discipline of sociology.

The visual in sociology

While the visual has always had a place in sociology, its use and analysis have fluctuated over the history of the discipline. More than a hundred years ago, the *American Journal of Sociology*, the flagship journal of the discipline, published a number of articles that used photos as data (Stasz 1979). According to Chaplin (1994: 201), the first manuscript of this type was F. Blackmar's 'The

Smoky Pilgrims', published in 1897. The study depicted poverty in rural Kansas using posed photographs. Yet, this early interest in the visual waned as the written word accompanied with numerical analysis became the dominant mode of sociological analysis. In a sense, statistical figures, charts, and tables became the visual centerpieces of professional sociological publications.

It is worth noting that this trend was not followed in the related discipline of anthropology. In fact, among the social sciences, anthropology is a leader of the use of pictorial and filmic materials. One of the more notable visual anthropological studies is Bateson and Mead's *Balinese Character: A Photographic Study* (1942). This study was exceptional in its use of photos as an integral part of the story. It juxtaposed text and the visual in a complementary way, so that one would enhance the meaning of the other. In the words of the authors,

> We are attempting a new method of stating the intangible relationship among different types of culturally standardised behavior by placing side by side mutually relevant photographs.... By the use of photographs, the wholeness of each piece of behavior can be preserved. (Bateson and Mead 1942: xii, as quoted in Harper 1994: 404)

Thus by showing a series of photos of a native ritual, for example, on one page and related text on the opposite page, Bateson and Mead encouraged their readers to see and read the story simultaneously.

Following their footsteps, a number of sociologists in recent decades have revived the interest in the visual. For example, in a 1974 article Becker (1974) called for bridging the gap between photography as an art form and photography as a mode of understanding and analyzing social reality. He also promoted greater appreciation for the role of social theory in producing and analyzing photographic images (cited in Harper 1994: 406). Becker subsequently published *Exploring Society Photographically* (1981), an edited book that follows a visual presentation style similar to that of Bateson and Mead.

Another notable sociologist that encouraged the use of visual analysis was Goffman, whose landmark sociological study, *Gender Advertisements* (1979), looked at how gender roles and expectations are reflected in magazine ads. Using over 500 photos, Goffman underlined the taken-for-granted nature of gender relations in Western societies. For example, he showed how magazine ads in the late 1970s, depicted men in active roles (doing things like helping patients or playing in sports), whereas the women were shown as mere spectators, passively watching the men's activities.

Any discussion of important works in visual sociology should also include Denzin's contributions. In books like *Images of Postmodern Society* (1991) and *Cinematic Society: The Voyeur's Gaze* (1995) he rejects the notion that cinematic representations are mere entertainment with no social value. Instead, he argues that we understand and express ourselves and our social settings through Hollywood films. According to Denzin, cinematic representations both describe social realities and mandate a way of seeing or accepting these realities. Consider, for example, his analysis of the movie *When Harry Met Sally*:

> The movie…is a 'Field Guide to Single Yuppies'….As such it takes a stand on and defines the following problematic terms; being single versus being married; sexuality and women's orgasms; love, sexuality, and friendship; life after divorce, or after breaking up with a lover. These terms are presented as obstacles….The solutions are gender specific. Women must not be single, must learn how to fake orgasms, so that males think they have sexual power…. Men, on the other hand, must have a woman who lets them think they can make them sexually happy. They need male friends to talk to, because women don't understand male sexuality. In this battle between the sexes, sex must be overcome, before love and friendship can be achieved. (Denzin 1995: 117)

In this analysis, the movie more than entertains; it mandates a way of thinking about male-female relationships. It becomes a how-to guide on heterosexual relations, constructing and describing the reality of how men and women should relate to one another. For Denzin, the cinematic representations become taken-for-granted truths. Indeed, I remember many of my friends citing *When Harry Met Sally* as empirical evidence for the inherently conflict-ual nature of heterosexual relationships. They would say, 'Didn't you see the movie? That's how we are.' Denzin's sociological analysis shows how cinematic images both construct and validate what we know about society.

As a whole, the visual is making a gradual comeback in sociology. It now has its own journals (e.g., *Visual Sociology* and *International Journal of Visual Sociology*) and annual conferences. However, as Ball and Smith (2001: 305) note, where anthropology has expanded its interest in the visual into moving images and ethnographic films, the field of sociology has more or less remained tied to still photography. The following section describes ways in which images could be conceptualized in social research.

Three facets of visual data

One way of assessing the research value of visual materials in qualitative socio-logy is to think about the different aspects of a picture or a movie. According to Rose, any visual piece can be judged along at least three dimensions: 1. the production; 2. the image; and 3. the audience (2001: 16).

Regarding production, we may begin by noting that visual images do not appear on the airways, in newspaper or magazines, or in theaters spontaneously. They have creators and a process of creation. As Rose puts it:

> All visual representations are made in one way or another, and the circumstances of their production may contribute towards the effect they have.
>
> Some writers argue this case very strongly. Some, for example, would argue that the *technologies* used in the making of an image determine its form, meaning and effect. Clearly visual technologies do matter to how an image looks and therefore to what it might do and what might be done to it. (2001: 17)

Let us evaluate the production differences between a still photo and a video-tape using the example of the terrorist bombing of the Twin Towers in

NewYork on September 11, 2001. Still pictures of the tragedy tend to provide snapshots of the moment of horror and people's reaction as they stare at or run away from the site.There is intensity in all the photos, and they are solemn and lurid. The moving images and videos, on the other hand, have a different quality. Perhaps, because we have seen many scenes like them in Hollywood motion pictures, they seem more incredible, like a violent scene from a movie that appears terrifying and unbelievable.

We should also consider that videographers and photographers have differing skills and operational needs. The photographer might look for a single image that tells 'the whole story,' whereas the videographer works on constructing a narrative that results from piecing together multiple action shots and sounds. Furthermore, the two bring into the field different material resources and organizational priorities. One might be taking pictures for a newspaper with a very small and politically partial readership, and the other could be videotaping for an undifferentiated mass market. Therefore, as Rose would suggest, the technique of production is a crucial part of what we see and is worthy of investigation in its own right.

Another elementary consideration in choosing and analyzing visual data is the image itself.The size, composition, color, texture and other characteristics of an image all figure into how it communicates its message. For example, a close-up of someone's face conveys a very different message than, let's say, a wide angle shot that shows the whole body. In fact, close-up images may be used deliberately to imply intensity or intimacy.Another example would be the use of bright red lighting in the background of a photo or a video. For many of us, that would suggest a sense of impending danger.Thus, in addition to the conditions and necessities of production, we can empirically study the properties of the image itself.

The third area of interest in researching visual materials, according to Rose, is the audience. Putting it simply, one cannot accurately evaluate the meaning of an image without knowledge about the audience.What a seventy-year-old sees in a music video is very different from the perceptions of an eighteen-year-old. The two have different levels and kinds of visual literacy and, therefore, would arrive at different conclusions about the meaning of the work. It is possible, then, to conduct a qualitative visual research purely based on variations in audience perceptions. No doubt, creators of commercial advertisements spend endless hours carefully assessing the effects of their ads on particular target audiences.

The varieties of visual data

We can categorize visual data in two ways: according to the medium's properties and according to whether they were generated by the researcher or some other agent.When attending to the medium' properties, we are essentially asking what kind of visual materials are we looking at? As stated earlier, the preferred choice for most sociologists has been still photos. One explanation for this tendency is that pictures are easier to reproduce for the purpose of print publications. Technologically, only recently have we begun to consider the possibility of multimedia presentations either on the internet or on compact disks utilizing moving images, stills, sound, and the written text all in the same context. It is reasonable to assume that the so-called electronic revolution could motivate sociologists to experiment with other visual media.

Videos and cinematic productions are a common source of data for sociologists. Naturally, working with these media requires a broader analytical framework. First, there is the issue of analyzing the effect of sound. For example, Chion's *Audio-Vision: Sound on Screen* (1994) is entirely devoted to how sound, or its absence, complements imagery. Another consideration, when working with moving pictures, is the internal logic and narrative coherence of the piece. That is, we could ask how different scenes are pieced together to tell the story.

When considering who created the visual data and for what purpose, the categories of interest will be 'researcher-generated' and 'found' images (Ball and Smith 2001). To put it simply, researchers either create their visual images of society, or they study works produced by someone else. Examples of researcher-generated materials include photos, films, or videos created by sociologists firsthand. The main advantage of producing your own visual images is that you can be in control of what, where, and how the work is shot or filmed. You pick the subject matter, the location and the style of the production. The drawbacks of this approach are that it is costly and very time-consuming. Alternatively, found images (e.g., movies and magazine adds) are widely accessible and inexpensive.

The range of visual data is by no means limited to moving and still pictures. Other options include animations, comics, cartoons, book illustrations, oil paintings, maps, or generally anything that is depicted visually. However, photos, videos and films appear to be the dominant sources of visual data.

How can we use visual data?

This section surveys some of the ways visual data is used in qualitative research. In particular, we will focus on the following approaches:

1 'Researcher-generated' visual material as the primary source of data and method of representing the research findings
2 The visual as a complement to the written text or as a way of telling ethnographic tales
3 The visual, particularly photographs, as a way of eliciting interviews and other data
4 Using 'found' photographic or filmic materials as secondary data for research and analysis (Adapted from Harper 2000 and Ball and Smith 2001: 314)

This is not intended as an exhaustive list. Certainly, one can combine these media to create new ones. Furthermore, rapid technological advances fore-shadow the creation of new visual media and modes of representation. With these points in mind, let us briefly review the items listed above.

Some social scientists, particularly in the field of anthropology, use videos and films to represent their research findings. A popular version of this approach is referred to as ethnographic films or videos. While informed by theoretical and methodological debates, such productions are not purely pedan-tic or illustrative of formal concepts. They combine aesthetic priorities with the auspices of scientific research to create works that inform general audiences about various social issues. For example, feminist ethnographic filmmakers have used the medium to raise public awareness about the plight of women and minorities in general.

> The camera, if used consciously as a tool to understand different interpretations of a culture and not as a tool to reproduce objective exotic proofs, can assist not only in reveal-ing to ourselves our own cognitive and cultural constructions, but it can also allow others to tell their stories in their own voice, with their own voices. (Kuehnast 1990: 26; as quoted in Vered 1993: 179)

For these ethnographers their visual productions are not necessarily an addition or a supplement to the written text. Instead, for them, ethnographic film is used as the primary means of communicating field observations to audiences.

Another use of the visual in the social sciences is as a complement to the written text, as discussed earlier in the case of Bateson and Mead's *Balinese Character* (1942). This type of work blends the visual with the textual. The visual in this sense becomes part data, part illustration, and part analysis. Establishing such a relationship between what the readers see and read is as much art as it is social science. Another example of this kind of work is Becker's *Exploring Society Photographically*, which uses photographs to examine social issues and realizes Becker's (1975) call for blurring the distinction between the art of photography and the science of sociology.

Similarly, Quinney (1996) uses photographs from his father's trip to California in the 1920s to tell the intimate, nostalgic story of his relationship with his father. Although Quinney's photographs are interspersed with written text, he places greater importance on the aesthetic quality of the visual. As he puts it, 'photographs are not to be subjected to 'scientific' and 'professional' discourse. Photography resists a language of analysis. The image speaks in silence. We give ourselves up to that which is beyond language and rational thought' (p. 381). Thus, the practice of combining the written text and the visual in sociology varies on a continuum ranging from aesthetic preferences to theoretical concerns about objectivity and scientific rigor.

The third item from our list at the start of this section has to do with the use of photographs as a way of eliciting interviews. In my research, I used photo-elicited interviews to examine college students' perceptions of race.

Four female respondents (two blacks and two whites) were provided with point-and-shoot cameras and instructed to take ten photographs from their everyday surroundings. The goal was for them to generate a visual answer to the question: 'What does racism mean to you?' Three of the subjects brought the cameras back after they had taken the pictures. The fourth never returned the camera or my phone calls about the project (I suppose that was her way of answering the question). After developing and printing the photos, I inter-viewed the research participants individually, with the photos laid out on the table. Each respondent elaborated on the meaning of their pictures. The following is an excerpt from one of these interviews. The photo being dis-cussed depicted a white waitress with her arm around a young black male (the manager of her restaurant).

Interviewer: With this picture, you said that it shows a major improve-
ment.... Do you think it shows that blacks are now upwardly
mobile, that they can have good jobs? Or are there still racial
barriers to their progress?

Respondent: They [blacks] are getting job offers. ... It's really neat to see
that he sees his potential [pointing to the black male in the
photo] to be a restaurant manager. I get the impression that
a lot of black people don't. First of all, maybe they don't want
to go to school. Maybe, they don't want to reach for what they
can do like working at McDonald's, which isn't a bad thing. If
they are really smart, they can go to school and do what they
want to do. And I am a person who's not going to stand in
their way of doing that.

Here the photo provided an avenue into the respondent's taken-for-granted assumptions about blacks. In particular, she articulates the view that the United States is a meritocracy in which blacks have opportunities, which, according to her, they choose not to fully exploit. From this perspective, the responsibility for racial inequality falls on the shoulders of minority group members themselves. This research strategy allowed me to develop the interviews and the probing questions around the respondents' photos and what their stated views were about race.

   The last item from the list refers to sociologists' analysis of 'found' visual materials, such as Goffman's (1979) analysis of magazine ads or Denzin's (1991; 1995) research on cinematic representations, both of which were described earlier. This method of using visual data could focus on topics such as culture and identity. Found visual data are plentiful and very inexpensive to obtain (you need only turn on your TV or flip through the pages of a magazine).

Analyzing the visual

The general topic of analyzing qualitative data (text, narrative, discourse, talk and so on) is addressed in Chapter 5, in this section, I offer a brief review of three orientations (content analysis, semiotics, and conversation analysis) that are especially suited for analyzing visual data.

Content analysis

This type of analysis in some respects follows the conventions of quantitative research. It makes use of random sampling techniques, coding schemes, and possibly numerical representations of visual data. Content analysis, as applied to visual data, brings together the qualitative interest in the substance of social experience and the quantitative emphasis on objective, unbiased research. As Ball and Smith put it:

> The objectivity of content analysis resides in the devising of precisely and clearly defined categories to apply to the material analyzed in accordance with explicitly formulated rules and procedures. In principle, different analysts using the same categories and rules would obtain identical results from their analysis of any given body of data; therein lies the reliability of the method. The rules of procedure serve to minimize the influence of the individual analyst's disposition and preconceptions. (1992: 21).

Typically, content analysis follows the steps listed below.

1   Define the research problem.
2   Select a source for the visual material to be used in the study.
3   Identify the categories or features that will be the focus of your research.
4   Sample documents from the sources previously defined.
5   Measure or count the occurrence of the pre-established categories. (Adapted from Ball and Smith 1992: 22–25)

In addition to generating numerical data, content analysis could also produce qualitative findings. A good example of grouping quantitative and qualitative techniques in content analysis of visual data is Lutz and Collins' *Reading the National Geographic* (1993), which explores the representations of non-Western cultures in the magazine *National Geographic*. Their analysis aims to reveal how the magazine's photographs reflect Western assumptions about the lifestyles of exotic people from faraway places. Here is how the authors describe their method of investigation:

> Our method consisted of randomly sampling one photograph from each of the 594 articles featuring non-Western people published in that period [between 1950-1986]. Each photo was coded independently by two people for twenty-two characteristics…. Although at first blush it might appear counterproductive to reduce the rich material in any photograph to a small number of codes, quantification does not preclude or substitute for qualitative analysis of the pictures. It does allow, however, discovery of patterns that are too subtle to be visible on casual inspection and protection against an unconscious search through the magazine for only those which confirm one's initial sense of what the photos say or do. (1993: 88–89)

As Rose (2001: 55) notes, Lutz and Collins's work shows that content analysis rules and procedures, if properly followed, can provide protections against bias and reveal patterns in the data that would go undetected using a less structured approach.

However, content analysis of visual data suffers the major shortcoming of primarily dealing with what is visible on the surface (Ball and Smith 1992). In Rose's words: 'Content analysis focuses on the image itself. But there are two other sites at which an image's meanings are made: the site of its production, and the site of its audiencing. Content analysis simply ignores both of these' (2001: 67). An orientation that is better suited for dealing with the cultural context of a visual image is semiotics.

Semiotics

When you look at a photo, what do you see? Say it's an image of a famous politician, like George W. Bush or Tony Blair. Typically, the photos of these leaders show them standing tall, dressed in suits with their national flags prominently displayed in the background. What information does such a picture convey on its surface? Perhaps that the leader is a man and he is dressed in professional attire. But as you look at the image of a middle-aged white male dressed in a suit, other meanings beyond the surface level might be evoked. For example, you might assume competence, honesty and professionalism about the person in the photo. Additionally, the flag might provoke a sense of patriotism in connection with the political figure, or the feeling that he is not just standing but standing *for* something (e.g., sovereignty or nationhood). Thinking about an image in this way is what *semiotics* (or semiology) is about.

Semiotics is about signs or objects that represent things other than themselves. In Silverman's words, 'Semiotics is the study of 'signs'. It shows how signs relate to one another in order to create and exclude particular meanings' (2001: 198). While the study of signs from this perspective began with an interest in words, for our purposes, I will limit the discussion to the analysis of photos. Going back to the example of a famous politician's photo, a semiotic analysis would suggest that the photo itself is a 'signifier,' or a culturally meaningful visual stimulus. What it stands for or symbolizes might be called the 'signified.' Drawing on the works of Barthes (1967), Silverman would say that the photo of our political leader both 'denotes' and 'connotes' a certain meaning. The meaning denoted on the surface is that a man dressed professionally is going about doing his job. The connoted meaning, on the other hand, is patriotism and nationalism, that the man in the photo represents and protects superior moral values that 'we' all believe in.

Thus, semiotics allows researchers to move conceptually between what is evident on the surface of a photo and its deeper cultural symbolism and meaning. In contrast with content analysis's detached scientific mission, the proponents of semiotics are ostensibly concerned about social inequalities and how they are rationalized through visual imagery (Rose 2001: 10). This emphasis is underlined in the following passage from an introductory book on social semiotics.

> In contemporary capitalist societies as in most other social formations there are inequalities in the distribution of power and other goods. As a result there are divisions in the social fabric between rulers and rules, exploiters and exploited…. In order to sustain these structures of domination, the dominant groups attempt to present the world in forms that reflect their own interests, the interests of their power. (Hodge and Kress 1988: 3; as quoted in Rose 2001: 70)

This way of analyzing images is not without its critics. One criticism against semiotics is 'a certain density of terminology' (Rose 2001: 73). The approach tends to be heavy on disciplinary jargon. Words like 'diegesis,' 'polysemy', and 'punctum' make the orientation inaccessible to unseasoned readers. The other problem, according to Rose, is that semiotics lacks methodological rigor: 'preference for detailed readings of individual images raises questions about the representativeness and replicability of its analyses' (p. 97).

Conversation analysis

Another way of analyzing visual data is using the techniques of conversation analysis and ethnomethodology (the study of how social reality is constructed and/or negotiated through everyday interaction and talk) (for a more detailed discussion of conversation analysis see Chapter 5). For example, Heath (1997) analyzes videotaped medical consultations to show how patients use body movements in combination with spoken words to convey the nature of their illness. The following excerpt from Heath's analysis describes how a woman physically demonstrates her difficulties with climbing stairs:

> As she [the patient] begins to step up [to the physician's desk] for the second time, she swings her hips towards the doctor…. As the hips move towards the doctor he looks up, turning to face the patient. It is as if the patient's movement elicits the reorientation by the doctor, encouraging him to temporarily abandon writing the prescription and transform the ways in which he is participating in the delivery of the [patient's] story…(1997: 194)

Heath supplements the above analysis with still images from his video-recordings that show a woman physically enacting her complaints within a few feet of a physician sitting at a desk.

For conversation analysts, visual images could further document how social reality is created through everyday interactions and talk. Again, as Heath puts it:

> the possibility of capturing aspects of audible and visual elements of *in situ* human conduct as it arises within its natural habitats provides researchers with unprecedented access to social actions and activities. With ethnomethodology and conversation analysis, the technology [videos and digital cameras] opens up the possibility of developing a sociology which begins to take visual as well as vocal aspects of human interaction and the physical environment seriously, as important topics for investigation and analysis. (1997: 198)

Following a similar ethnomethodological approach, Suchman (1987) uses video-recordings to examine problems associated with human-machine inter-actions. In particular, she videotaped how people interact with copy machines to underscore the many gaps between the users' orientations toward their tasks and the way artificial-intelligence devices are programmed to help them. Suchman argues that such machines assume their users follow a specific plan or predetermined course of action. In practice, however, users approach these devices more fluidly; they develop their plans for using them as they perform daily tasks. The fundamental problem is that the machines' step-by-step instructions are often incongruent with the dynamic ways in which people go about using tools to do their work.

There are many other ways of analyzing visual data. Your choice of methods and analysis will most likely depend on your theoretical leanings, the type of material you are working with, and other logistical considerations, such as time and financial cost. The next section deals with the more practical side of doing visual work, particularly in regard to photography and videography.

Technical considerations in doing photographic research

I want to end this chapter by offering you several tips that might save you hours of agonizing over the question 'What went wrong?' This technical advice is intended to help you shoot better photos or videos. Of course, the idea of 'better' is relative. Sometimes, you might decide, for very good theoretical reasons, that distortions (e.g., the subject matter being blurred or not well-lit) are research findings in their own right and need not be corrected. With visual sociology, what constitutes a 'good' photo or video is determined by your theoretical and methodological parameters. For example, if you are doing photo-elicited interviews using pictures taken by respondents, everything about the way they view their social world is empirically relevant, including defects caused by the way they use the camera. Another example of meaning-ful distortion is when ethnographic filmmakers shoot their subjects from the neck down to hide their identity.

Having said that, regardless of your particular visual strategy, you should be familiar with the technical aspects of the equipment, especially if you are gen-erating your own visual data. As Harper states:

> Becoming a visual ethnographer means becoming conscious of the potential to make visual statements by knowing how the camera interprets social reality. This means learn-ing how cameras work, making the technical decisions that, in fact, create the photograph self-consciously, and relegating the automatic camera to the wastebasket. (2000: 724)

While Harper's stand on automatic cameras might sound a bit radical, his overall message of 'learning how cameras work' is sound advice for anyone interested in the field of visual sociology. This section helps you with this task by describing 1. the different types of photographic cameras (viewfinder, single lens reflex and digital) and 2. the factors that affect how the pictures come out (aperture control, shudder speed, composition, lighting, etc.). I end the section with a few remarks about the use of video equipment in qualitative research.

Viewfinder, single lens reflex and digital cameras

There are three basic types of cameras: viewfinder, single lens reflex (SLR) and digital. The first two work with 35mm film (a popular choice for most photographers named after the length of each frame in millimeters). With viewfinder cameras, a common variety of which is the automatic point-and-shoot, the image that you see through the viewfinder before you take the picture is not what the camera lens sees. The problem with this system is even when you think you have framed the subject matter perfectly in the viewfinder, the lens might see the image differently from what you want to record. The result is that important features of the subject matter are 'cut off' in the finished product. The solution is simple: when working with a point-and-shoot, always leave a little extra space around the edges. Don't frame your subject too tightly because you might lose a limb or a head, as it were.

The other type of film-equipped cameras, SLRs, gives you more control over the production process. An SLR's most important advantage over its viewfinder counterpart is that what you see is what you get – the images you see through the opening on top of the camera is what the lens sees. Thus, the final product will appear as it was framed. Another advantage of this type of camera is that it often provides you a choice of lenses to work with. For example, if you want to bring the subject matter closer, you can take the standard lens off and mount a telephoto one on the camera (a telephoto lens works like a telescope, it brings distant objects closer). Additionally, SLRs are more likely to give you control over other features of the camera such as shudder speed and aperture opening, two important camera controls which I will discuss in more detail later in this section.

In addition to viewfinders and SLRs, digital cameras are becoming more widely available at lower prices and with more features. While the initial cost of a digital camera might be slightly higher than its counterparts, in the long run, it more than pays for itself in savings from the cost of film, developing, and prints. The more advanced digital models give you all the control and precision of SLRs. Furthermore, digitally taken photographs (or digitalized images in general) can be enhanced or altered considerably after the image is recorded. Many come with computer software that could correct lighting and color problems after the picture is taken. Digital images can also easily be shared with colleagues via the internet and email. However, this type of camera has at least one major drawback. Most digital images don't produce clear prints, especially when they are enlarged. Fortunately, this problem is being solved by the more advanced, high-resolution models.

Camera controls and other considerations

Photography literally means writing with light. The appearance of a photo is determined by the amount of light that is registered on film: the more light the brighter the picture, the less light the darker. Point-and-shoot cameras don't let you manipulate the amount of light that enters the camera. At best, you are provided with an automatic flash that solves the problem of taking pictures in dimly-lit places. Alternatively, SLRs are packed with little knobs and buttons for controlling how much light enters the camera. The two main camera controls are aperture and shutter speed. The former determines the light coming in through the lens, and the latter sets the speed at which the shutter (a small curtain inside the camera) opens and closes. The longer the shutter is open or the wider your aperture, the more light reaches the film. Suppose you want to take a picture of a building at night, and you don't want to use a flash because it distorts the natural lighting. The solution is to use a wide aperture opening and a slow shutter speed to allow enough light into the camera to expose the film. On the other hand, if you are taking a picture of a man standing outside on a sunny day, a smaller aperture and faster shutter speed are the logical choices because you need less light.

Other basic components of a 'good' photo are composition and framing. Composition basically means arranging the subject matter in a way that best communicates your message. As semiologists would suggest, this is as much about cultural convention as it is about aesthetics. For example, family photos of Middle Easterners might show the father, or the patriarch, in the center. Be aware of the significance of composition and use it effectively. In regard to framing, the same principles apply. Make deliberate choices about how you frame a picture and what angle you shoot it from. For example, if you want to depict the perspective of a person who is in a wheelchair, you might want to stoop down and shoot your photos from the waist level to emphasize the visual angle of the disabled.

Another factor to keep in mind when working with photographic equipment is your choice of film. There are three considerations here. First, decide if you want to work with color or black and white film. Second, consider whether you want to work with slide or print film. Slides can be projected on a large screen and thus shown to a larger audience, whereas prints cannot be displayed with the same ease. Lastly, take into account the speed of the film. This is indicated on the film as ISO. The faster the film, the better you are able to capture or freeze an image in motion. Also, faster films work better in darker conditions and reduce the need for a flash.

A few notes on videography

Video technology has steadily improved in the past few decades. The trend has been in the direction of giving you more control over the recording process and making the camera (or the camcorder as it is sometimes called) smaller in size. Working with video cameras is somewhat similar to the use of still cameras. The same concerns about manipulating the lighting, composition and framing apply here. As far as the choice of film is concerned, keep in mind that videotapes do not last forever, they degenerate with repetitive use. The metallic coating on the surface of a video tape wears off a bit each time it is shown. A good practice is to always make backup copies of your original tapes. If you are going to display your work repeatedly, use your backup, so that the original remains intact. It is also important to purchase quality film, cheaper video tapes wear out faster.

Another important consideration with video tapes is sound. A standard camcorder microphone is 'omni-directional.' That means within an approximately 360-degree range, the microphone picks up just about every sound. The problem is when you are doing an interview on the street, for example, in addition to your respondent's voice, you are recording all the background noises (e.g., cars driving by and other people speaking). This type of sound interference could mask the voice of the respondent, which means you could end up in the very frustrating situation of not being able to hear your best interview. If you plan to use a camcorder for interview purposes, you have at least three options. One is to conduct the interview in a studio, or at least a very quiet room. Alternatively, you can use special equipment such as a shotgun mike. This is a microphone that can be pointed in specific direction and will pick up only the sound emanating from that source. Another option is a lapel microphone, which could be cordless or wired and attaches to the speaker's shirt or jacket.

CHAPTER SUMMARY

This chapter explored how qualitative sociologists have incorporated the visual into their research. I began by considering the idea of a 'visual culture' and its implications for research. From this perspective, the visual is approached as a powerful medium that constructs reality and ways of seeing for audiences in various cultural contexts. I then discussed the history of visual research in sociology beginning with the earlier interest in the late 1800s to the more recent work by Becker, Goffman, and Denzin. The next part of the chapter focused on visual data and its analysis. We discussed the three dimensions of visual data (production, the image, and the audience) and went on to classify visual data as either researcher-generated or found. In addition, we examined how the visual could be used as: primary data, secondary data, a complement to the written text, or a way of eliciting interviews. Next, I presented three ways of analyzing this type of data: content analysis, semiotics, and conversation analysis. I suggested that content analysis tends to be more concerned about sampling and measurement, whereas semiotics takes a more reflexive approach, analytically moving between the qualities of the image and its cultural context. With conversation analysis, the goal is to use recorded images to understand how social reality is constructed in everyday interaction and through talk. The chapter ended with a review of some technical and practical considerations about shooting photographs and videos, the gist of which was that you should familiarize yourself with the equipment before embarking on your research.

SUGGESTED READINGS

A relatively accessible and thorough read on the use and interpretation of visual media is Gillian Rose's *Visual Methodologies* (2001). Ball and Smith's *Analyzing Visual Data* (2001) is another work that introduces the basic components of visual analysis. For a detailed discussion on the status of the visual in the discipline of sociology see Chaplin's *Sociology and Visual Representation* (1994). For those interested in an overview of the field of cultural studies, Evans and Hall's edited volume *Visual Culture: The Reader* (2000) is packed with classic and contemporary articles on the topic.

EXERCISE 4.1

OBJECTIVE: To apply visual analysis to understanding how gender is portrayed in magazine ads.

DESCRIPTION: The source of data for this study could be pictures from popular magazines in which men and women are shown in the same frame. If possible, instead of choosing your pictures at will, select every other suitable photo and photocopy it for future reference. Write a short paragraph in answer to each of the following questions about social patterns that could be detected in your photos:

1 Where are the women placed in the ads relative to the men? For example, are they standing behind the men or kneeling in front of them?
2 Are there any gender distinctions in the activities shown in the photos? Are the men and women involved in the same type of jobs or tasks? Is one gender more likely to be physically active and the other watching the performance?
3 Sociologically speaking, what can you infer from these differences in spatial positioning and activities?

5

Data Analysis

Imagine a group of graduate students in a course seminar. A doctoral candidate is presenting data from his dissertation in progress. A field-interview extract, projected on a screen at the end of the room, is the focus of everyone's attention. It is about an exchange with a homeless man outside of an emergency shelter who is asking the researcher to relay to the staff his complaints about being unfairly treated.

Interviewer: Well, I don't work there anymore... I just come here and do
my interviews and work as a volunteer, so I'm not on the
staff. So I'm not trying to protect anybody, but, uh—
Respondent: But you do see?
Interviewer: I'm not blind.
Respondent: You see? You hear?
Interviewer: I'm not blind and I'm not deaf.

The doctoral student thinks this is an example of moral ambivalence in
fieldwork, one of those cases where there is no right answer, but some of his
fellow students see it differently. One of them suggests that this is a case of good
rapport. He argues, 'He's telling you he trusts you! He's bonding with you.'
Another says, 'Your situation makes a good case for "action research," getting
involved in respondents' lives and making a difference.' Finally, a cynical interpretation of the data comes from an older student who suggests, 'He's trying to
take advantage of you. You gotta be careful about that sort of thing in the field.'
The doctoral student decides, in the final analysis, to leave the excerpt out of
his dissertation. 'Hard to fit into my theoretical paradigm,' he writes in his
research memos about the exchange.

The graduate students described above are involved in *data analysis*, or the
interpretive activity of making sense of human artifacts by conceptually connecting them with other meaningful information. This task is like connecting
the dots, or telling your audience how the pieces of information fit together.
It would be misleading to suggest that data analysis is a separate phase of the
research process. In many ways, you begin analysis as you collect data. From the
very start qualitative researchers:

* think and write about how one set of observations relates to another
* provide tentative explanations for these relationships
* pose new questions.

This chapter does not present data analysis as a distinct portion of qualitative
research, rather I hope to show how we could make sense of sociological data,
irrespective of when data analysis formally begins. Using the concepts of constructionism and objectivism, the chapter opens by emphasizing the relationship between theory and data analysis. Next, basic steps in analyzing qualitative
data, such as data reduction and display, will be reviewed (Huberman and Miles
1994). The bulk of the chapter then focuses on the assumptions and practical
applications of the following approaches to qualitative data analysis: content
analysis, narrative analysis, and conversation and discourse analysis. This is followed by a brief discussion of how sociologists evaluate their research findings
(i.e., reliability and validity). The chapter ends with a summary of the advantages and disadvantages of the use of computer software programs in qualitative data analysis.

Theoretical considerations: objectivism and constructionism

Theory plays a foundational role in how qualitative data is analyzed. For some sociologists, the word 'theory' has a formal definition; it refers to a set of philosophical assumptions about the social world attributed to an intellectual father figure like Karl Marx or Max Weber. Examples of formal sociological theories include structural functionalism, symbolic interactionism, and conflict theory. Numerous volumes have been devoted to the study of social theories and it is not my intention to summarize these works here, but it is worthwhile to consider how our understanding of social reality shapes the research questions we ask.

In particular, let us briefly examine the relationship between qualitative data analysis and the two perspectives of objectivism and constructionism. Objectivism assumes that information about the social world could be analyzed to reveal a reality or social structure beyond the data itself, whereas constructionism approaches data analysis as a way of showing how the data, text, or talk is organized and created through social interaction. To compare the two perspectives, let us begin by considering an extract from a speech given by a formerly homeless man to a group of college students.

> I didn't have too much hope for a couple of years. I was alone with my problem. Today, I know I'm not alone. There are a lot of people who care. And by their caring I care.... I would not wish this on anyone but I'm glad it happened to me, a lesson about life and a lesson about myself. (Marvasti 1998: 177)

How do you read this passage? What does it say to you? From an objectivist viewpoint, it tells us about a man who had some problems – though from this excerpt it is not clear what those problems were. We also learn about a man who is grateful for those caring people who helped him get off the streets, to transform his identity from being homeless to something better, presumably 'a normal citizen.' I suppose we can collect tens of similar accounts from formerly homeless people and glean some kind of pattern from them. For example, if they all spoke of 'caring others' as a crucial part of their recovery, we can conclude that to end homelessness, we need a lot of caring people. This in turn would lead for the establishment of social programs that encourage concerned citizens to get involved in helping the needy and so forth, which is a perfectly legitimate interpretation of the data, but it is not the only one.

Let us now analyze the same piece of data from a constructionist perspective. Viewing the data this way, one of the first things I notice about this speech is that it has two complementary parts. The first part tells the audience how things were before. He was 'alone' and without 'too much hope.' That was then. The audience is now ready to hear the second part, which is about how things are now: 'Today, I know I'm not alone,' followed by the declaration 'I'm glad it happened to me …' The reason this man's statement about being 'glad' to have experienced homelessness makes sense to us in a morally acceptable way is because of its redemption format. He can afford to be glad now because he is not homeless anymore. To have a complete redemption narrative you need both parts of the story (i.e., the troubles *then* and the way things are *now*). If we focused on either part alone, we would miss the point of this moral tale of recovery. I did this analysis using similar stories and concluded that to tell a tale of redemption, the speaker must first expose the stigma of his or her past before speaking about accomplishments of the present (Marvasti 1998).

What is the practical point of this finding? Well, here is where constructionism gets a bad reputation. Certainly, I cannot speak of the constructionist analysis with the same air of moral authority implied in the objectivist approach, which points to a much more impressive project of helping needy people by creating networks of caring others. What I can show through my analysis is how people, 'deviant people' in this case, use their stigma to present themselves in a positive light. So, rather than hiding them, social outcasts sometimes put forth their stigmatized selves. I can go on to argue that they are not as 'helpless' as they might seem at first glance. On the contrary, they are intelligent, thoughtful people. Granted, this analysis does not put food on the table, so to speak, but it does keep us from making stereotypical assumptions about people.

I do not mean to suggest that somehow constructionism is more intellectually rigorous than objectivism, but I simply want to illustrate that the same data can be read or analyzed from differing perspectives, each making its own reasonable argument about what is relevant about the speech. My larger purpose here is to suggest that data analysis is inseparable from theory and theorizing. As you analyze your data, keep in mind that you are explicitly or implicitly applying a way of seeing, a particular analytical vocabulary and related insights. To illustrate this point, let us consider a theoretical model that was specifically developed to explain the merits of a qualitative approach to social research.

Grounded theory

The notion of 'grounded theory' was originally developed by Glaser and Strauss in *The Discovery of Grounded Theory* (1964), which argued qualitative analysis could systematically generate concepts and theories based on observational data. This is what is known as an inductive or grounds–up approach to data analysis. One begins with general observations and through an ongoing analytical process creates conceptual categories that explain the topic under study. As Glaser and Strauss state:

> A grounded theory that is faithful to everyday realities of a substantive area is one that has been carefully *induced* from diverse data.... Only in this way will the theory be closely related to the daily realities (what is actually going on) of substantive areas, and so be highly applicable to dealing with them. (pp. 238–39, as cited in Strauss and Corbin 1994)

Glaser and Strauss's original conceptualization of grounded theory has undergone some changes (see Strauss and Corbin 1990 and 1994 for a revised interpretation of grounded theory). While numerous variations of the original idea exist, as Charmaz notes, they all have the following components in common:

(a) simultaneous data collection and analysis; (b) pursuit of emergent themes through early data analysis, (c) discovery of basic social processes within the data, (d) inductive construction of abstract categories that explain and synthesize these processes, (e) sampling to refine the categories through comparative processes, and (f) integration of categories into a theoretical framework that specifies causes, conditions, and consequences of the studied processes. (2002: 677)

Grounded theory gives special importance to two ideas. The first is the emphasis on theorizing close to the data. Sociologists who use this approach are encouraged to keep their analysis within the boundaries of their data. This means abstract concepts should remain grounded in empirical observations, and if necessary, be revised to reflect changes in the data. The other central theme of grounded theory is a commitment to the development of theories. Within this orientation the word 'theory' has a specific meaning. For traditional grounded theory researchers:

Theory consists of *plausible* relationships proposed among *concepts* and *sets of concepts*. (Though only plausible, its plausibility is to be strengthened through continued research.) Without concepts, there can be no propositions, and thus no cumulative scientific (systematically theoretical) knowledge based on these plausible and testable propositions. (Strauss and Corbin 1994: 278)

Grounded theorists generate two types of theories: substantive and formal. Substantive theories explain a particular aspect of social life, such as why or how juvenile delinquency or teen pregnancy happens. Formal theories, while informed by their substantive siblings, take the level of explanation a few notches higher; they explain social issues at a higher level of abstraction (such as a particular theory of social inequality that explains a wide range of social problems).

As Strauss and Corbin acknowledge, 'Researchers using grounded theory have undoubtedly been much influenced by contemporary intellectual developments, including ethnomethodology, feminism, political economy, and varieties of postmodernism' (1994: 276). In other words, there is more than one way of doing grounded theory analysis. The following discussion presents a type of grounded theory that is built around a more interpretive or constructionist orientation.

A constructionist grounded theory

According to Charmaz (2002), constructionist grounded theory views data collection and analysis as tools that help researchers produce tentative

TABLE 5.1   *Comparison of objectivist and constructionist grounded theory perspectives on qualitative research*

	Objectivist	**Constructionist**
Data analysis	The data and its analysis reveal real meaning about real facts: 'Let the facts speak for themselves.'	The data and its analysis are social constructions: 'Whose facts, for what purpose and in what setting?'
Research method/technique	Strict adherence to preestablished methods such as coding techniques	Sensitive to how contextual factors (e.g., time, place and culture) influence the research process
Researcher role	Researcher must remain objective so that the facts emerge untainted	Allows for subjective interpretations by the researcher and the respondents to be part of the analysis

explanations about the social construction of reality. In objectivist versions of grounded theory, meaning is something to be 'discovered' in the data. Discovery means something akin to prospecting for gold nuggets of facts in a riverbed of data. A constructionist grounded theory, on the other hand, places emphasis on how the data and its analysis are products of social interaction. The focus is on the process of social interaction and how it creates meaning. Table 5.1 summarizes Charmaz's distinctions between an objectivist and constructionist grounded theory.

Given its theoretical position, constructionist grounded theory analyzes qualitative data as follows. The first step, is coding the data using 'sensitizing concepts' (Blumer 1969). A sensitizing concept is basically a working tool for analysis. It is not set in stone and can be revised or elaborated to fit the nuances of the topic being studied (you are not bound to it for life, if it doesn't work, get rid of it). Charmaz suggests that before settling on a particular set of concepts you should ask the following questions:

(a) What, if anything does the concept illuminate about these data? (b) How, if at all, does the concept specifically apply here? (c) Where does the concept take the analysis? As researchers answer such questions, they make decisions about boundaries and usefulness of the sensitizing concept. (2002: 684)

With practical and theoretically self-conscious definitions of concepts, the researcher can proceed to the two phases of coding: 'initial' and 'selective or focused coding' (Charmaz 2002). During *initial coding*, the goal is to peruse the data for meaningful categories or themes. Table 5.2 is an example of Charmaz's initial coding of data from an in-depth interview with a woman who suffers from chronic illness and pain.

As seen in Table 5.2, initial coding seems a bit like free association. You put down a series of concepts that come to mind as you read through the data. Initial coding centers around basic questions like 'What is this about?' or 'What does this text communicate and how?'

TABLE 5.2   *Example of initial coding from Charmaz's research on chronic illness*

Initial coding	Interview statement
Recounting the events	And so I went back to work on March 1, even
Going against medical advice	though I wasn't supposed to. And
	then when I got there, they had a long
Being informed of changed rules	meeting and they said I could no longer
Suffering as a moral status	rest during the day. The only time I
Accounting for legitimate rest time	rested was at lunch time, which was my
Distinguishing between 'free' and work time	time, we were closed. And she said, my
	supervisor, said I couldn't do that
Receiving an arbitrary order	anymore, and I said, 'It's my time, you
Making moral claim	can't tell me I can't lay down.'

Source: Adapted from Charmaz 2002: 685

Initial coding is followed by more theoretically sensitive categorization of the data, or *focused coding*. Charmaz notes, 'In selective or focused coding, the researcher adopts frequently reappearing initial codes in sorting and synthesizing large amounts of data. Focused codes are more abstract, general, and, simultaneously, more incisive than the initial codes…' (2002: 686). Focused coding broadens the concepts' level of abstraction while simultaneously expanding the range of their application (i.e, they become more theoretical and apply to a broader range of observations). Table 5.3 shows how Charmaz applies focused coding to the analysis of the previous extract from her research.

In this example, the general or focused codes basically allow the researcher to reduce the possible universe of meanings, moving from a large number of initial codes to a smaller, more manageable set. Also note that in her coding Charmaz tends to give preference to what she calls 'action codes,' or categories that direct our attention to the ongoing nature of social interaction or social phenomena. In her words, 'I try to make action in the data visible by looking at the data in action. Hence I use terms such as *going, making, having*, and *seeing*. Using action codes helps the researcher to remain specific and not take leaps of fancy' (p. 685). In summary, other general points to consider about coding, according to Charmaz, include:

- remaining empirically sensitive and flexible throughout the research process (don't be dogmatic about your codes; if they don't fit the data, try a different set of concepts);
- revising or supporting your coding strategy by referring to the academic literature on the topic and collecting more data;
- allowing for the possibility that your coding strategy may raise more research questions and call for more data collection.

Charmaz also recommends the use of 'memo writing' as a way of elaborating on your analytical categories and actually beginning the task of writing the research report. A research memo is a statement of your analytical judgment and interpretation of the data. It is where you begin to say things like 'I think

TABLE 5.3   *Example of focused coding from Charmaz's research on chronic illness*

Focused coding	Interview statement
Going against medical advice	And so I went back to work on March 1, even though I wasn't supposed to. And then when I got there, they had a long meeting and they said I could no longer
Suffering as a moral status	rest during the day. The only time I rested was at lunch time, which was my time, we were closed. And she said, my supervisor, said I couldn't do that anymore, and I said, 'It's my time, you
Making moral claim	can't tell me I can't lay down.'

Source: Adapted from Charmaz 2002: 685

X is related to Y because ...' Below is a research memo that shows how Charmaz elaborates on her concept of 'suffering as a moral status':

> Suffering is a profoundly moral status as well as a physical experience. Stories of suffering reflect and redefine that moral status. With suffering comes moral rights and entitlements as well as moral definitions – when suffering is deemed legitimate. Thus the person can make certain moral claims **and** have certain moral judgments conferred upon him or her. (pp. 687–88)

To recap, constructionist grounded theory progresses from a broad categorization of the data (initial coding) to more abstract concepts (focused codes) using research memos, which provide the raw material for the final report.

The theoretical perspectives discussed so far are associated with a number of sub-fields and methods of analysis within the realm of qualitative research. In the remainder of this chapter, the focus will be on several other ways of analyzing qualitative data. We begin by first reviewing the basic steps that all forms of qualitative data analysis have in common.

Doing qualitative analysis: the basic steps

Regardless of your theoretical perspective, all forms of qualitative analysis seem to be based on three procedures: 'data reduction,' 'data display,' and 'conclusion: drawing/ verifying' (Huberman and Miles 1994). Note that these steps are not mutually exclusive and separate from other dimensions of research. Most qualitative sociologists would agree that as a whole, data collection, analysis, and writing are interrelated parts that do not occur in clearly distinct and progressive stages. The different phases of research and writing often proceed concurrently and inform each other. As Coffey and Atkinson state:

> The process of analysis should not be seen as a distinct stage of research; rather, it is a reflexive activity that should inform data collection, writing, further data collection, and

so forth. Analysis is not, then, the last phase of the research process. It should be seen as part of the research design and of the data collection. The research process, of which analysis is one aspect, is a cyclical one. (1996: 6)

Thus qualitative analysis should be viewed as a dynamic and inventive process. Having said that, some degree of organization is essential. The following discussion of Huberman and Miles's (1994) organizational scheme helps the novice researcher bring coherence and manageability to the analysis of his or her data.

Reducing your data

It is very likely that your research project is going to generate more data than you will use in your final write up. For example, for my doctoral research I conducted over fifty interviews and generated many pages of field notes over a three-year period. The two sources of data combined added to nearly 1,000 pages of transcriptions, research memos, and notes. By contrast, the final product of my research, the dissertation, was about 250 pages. So I had to edit the data, summarize it, and make it presentable. A finished qualitative report is like a well-edited movie, much of the filmmaker's raw footage ends up on the editing room floor.

We have to reduce our data to make things more manageable. Analyzing a small size of key information is much easier than poring through thousands of pages back and forth. In fact, we begin to zoom in on some segments of data from the very moment we pose a research question. The selective attention to the data starts when we decide to study a particular aspect of social life from a range of infinite topics. As Huberman and Miles note:

> With *data reduction*, the potential universe of data is reduced in an anticipatory way as the researcher chooses a conceptual framework, research questions, cases, and instruments. Once actual field notes, interviews, tapes, or other data are available, data summaries, coding, finding themes, clustering, and writing stories are all instances of further data selection and condensation. (1994: 429)

Data reduction is not necessarily about what you do after you collect your data, but it, directly or indirectly, is infused throughout the entire research process. Given the unlimited range of sociological topics, as researchers, we are always reducing the potential universe of data when we choose one topic over another. For me, my interest in social inequality was the first step in reducing relevant data. Narrowing my topic to homelessness represented another reductive phase. Going to an emergency shelter was yet another way of zooming in on my data, and so on.

Displaying your data

Hubeman and Miles's (1994) notion of *data display* roughly involves using textual representations of your data for the purpose of selecting segments that best illustrate your concepts of interest. Typically, this includes the following:

- carefully reading and rereading data transcriptions
- making notes in the margins (sometimes referred to as 'research memos')
- highlighting important passages or themes as representations of particular concepts.

The objective is to gradually transform a seemingly chaotic mess of raw data into a recognizable conceptual scheme. For most sociologists, the medium of choice for display and selection purposes is paper; however, some might be more comfortable viewing their data on a computer screen. In fact, there are some computer software programs, such as NUD★IST or NVivo, that allow you to draw diagrams and write research memos on the margins of your computer screen (some general comments on the use of software in qualitative research are offered at the end of this chapter).

Drawing conclusions

This last step in the analysis involves making meaningful statements about how your data illustrates your topic of interest. As Huberman and Miles note, this step involves 'drawing meaning from displayed data' (1994: 429). The word 'drawing' should be taken quite literally here: you draw the relevant meaning, structure or processes out of the data based on the type of analysis you choose. What meanings should be drawn from the analysis? The answer depends on your disciplinary orientation. For example, we recognize certain studies as being sociological based on the way the researchers made sense of their data, or the particular meanings they drew from their data using a sociological orientation.

In the following pages, I present an overview of a number of approaches to analyzing qualitative data with an emphasis on sociological interpretations. Admittedly, the space allotted to each perspective is brief. My goal is to introduce simply the broad contours to the novice researcher. We should keep in mind that the full treatment of any of the following qualitative approaches to data analysis could fill several volumes.

Content analysis

This section begins with a definition of content analysis and goes on to discuss two ways of analyzing *text*, which for our purposes refers to recorded information about social life in the form of visual images, published written material, or transcribed interviews. The section ends with a summary of the basic steps in doing content analysis.

Text as a reflection of public opinion

According to Bauer (2000), content analysis involves 'Systematic classification and counting of text units [to] distill a large amount of material into a short description of some of its features' (pp. 132–33). For qualitative researchers, the instant appeal of this approach is the convenience it offers in simplifying and reducing large amounts of data into organized segments. Using content analysis, you can translate the content of thousands of pages of religious writings, for example, into a few common themes, such as 'the struggle between good and evil.'

Bauer states one way of interpreting textual data is to examine it as a 'medium of expression' that reflects a people's culture and practices. He argues that texts:

> contain records of event, values, rules and norms, entertainment, and traces of conflict and argument. … [Content analysis] allows us to construct indicators of worldviews, values, attitudes, opinions, prejudices and stereotypes, and compare these across communities. In other words, … [content analysis] is public opinion research by other means. (2000: 133–34)

From this perspective, texts could be used to make inferences about public attitudes. For example, many years ago I was interested in South Floridians' attitudes toward bilingualism, which in this case refers to the official recognition and use of the Spanish language in addition to English. In 1980, a conservative political group in Dade County (a large municipality in South Florida with a sizeable Hispanic population) organized a referendum vote to declare the county officially monolingual. Their proposal was as follows:

> The expenditure of county funds for the purpose of utilizing any language other than English, or promoting any culture other than that of the United States, is prohibited. All county governmental meetings, hearings, and publications shall be in the English language only. (Stein 1980: 23A)

This 'English-only' proposal, which was eventually voted into law, was intended to reverse earlier legislation that had declared the area officially bilingual in 1973. That earlier measure stated the following as reasons for promoting bilingualism:

> To aid the Spanish-speaking population in achieving the goals they have traveled so far to share … to enter more easily the mainstream of American way of life … to promote a mutually prosperous interchange of ideas as well as closer affinity with these citizens. (Stein 1980: 23A)

My research question was: What was the public's rationale for supporting the anti-bilingual initiative? To collect data for my analysis, I perused archives of a local newspaper, *The Miami Herald*, in search of editorials, letters to the editor, and articles that argued in favor of the proposed law. The use of the archives was necessary because I started my research in 1990, ten years after much of the material was originally published. Below are two examples of texts supporting the anti-bilingual legislation:

> The ordinance is not a hate thing.… The American, the English-speaking people would like to have this community back the way it was. They would like to have their language back. (Emmy Schafer, a South Florida resident, quoted in Arocha 1980: 3B)

TABLE 5.4   *Classification of The Miami Herald articles, editorials and letters to the editor published in 1980 in support of anti-bilingualism in Dade County, Florida*

Theme	Example	Number	Percentage
Patriotism	To be *true* Americans immigrants must speak English.	6	17
Assimilation	America is a 'melting pot' and English is the 'common element.'	11	31
Polarization	Bilingualism polarizes members of society.	5	14
Voters' rights	Voters have the right to vote on anything they choose including antibilingualism.	4	11
Public nuisance	Immigrants who speak Spanish in public places disturb native English speakers.	4	11
Job discrimination	Employers might discriminate against English-only speakers by hiring bilinguals.	3	9
Non-official Bilingualism	Bilingualism could exist, but it shouldn't be officially recognized.	2	6
		35	100

The Proponents of bilingualism invariably insist loudly that this [Dade County] is a bilingual community and bilingualism is not going to go away. If this is so, why does the tag 'official' have to be attached? (Cajacob 1980: 6A)

I analyzed a total of thirty five letters to the editor in search of themes that served as rhetorical explanations for supporting anti-bilingualism. These themes are displayed in Table 5.4.

This simple example of content analysis explores public opinion by summarizing related texts into explanatory categories. Using a small sample, it shows seven ways in which South Floridians accounted for their desire to make the area officially monolingual. In addition to analyzing text as a reflection of public opinion, content analysis could also be used to show how public opinion is shaped. The next discussion presents this line of thinking.

Text as a cause of public opinion

Another way of analyzing the content of textual material is to treat it as an independent variable, or as something that causes another factor to change.

TABLE 5.5   *First and last name use in tennis commentary, totals*

	First only	**Last only**	**First and last**
Women	304 (52.7)	166 (28.8)	107 (18.5)
Men	44 (7.8)	359 (69.8)	127 (22.4)

Note: Numbers in parentheses represent percentages.
Source: Adapted from Messner et al. 1993: 128

Specifically, some content analysts approach the text as causing or creating public opinion. In Bauer's words, the text in this fashion is viewed as a '*medium of appeal*: an influence on people's prejudices, opinions, attitudes, and stereotypes' (2000: 134). Looking at text from this perspective means searching for themes that could be connected with certain cultural practices or attitudes (i.e., X, the textual representation, constructs Y, the public opinion).

Following this approach, Messner et al. (1993) show how the verbal commentaries from sports broadcasts construct or reinforce traditional gender roles for male and female athletes. The researcher's techniques for the study is described as follows:

> First we recorded the basketball games and tennis matches on videotape and conducted a pilot study [a preliminary analysis involving a small portion of the data] of the tapes. The pilot study had two outcomes. First, the research design was fine-tuned and a preliminary list of specific questions was constructed. Next, we developed standardized ways of analyzing the verbal commentary. Then, the research assistant viewed all of the tapes and compiled a detailed record of her observations. Next, all of the tapes were independently viewed and analyzed by one of the investigators, who then added her written analysis to that of the research assistant. Finally, the data were compiled and analyzed by two investigators, using both sets of written descriptions of the tapes and by viewing portions of the tapes once again. (1993: 125)

One of the interesting findings from this study is that the sportscasters sometimes referred to the female athletes as 'girls'; however, their male counterparts were *never* referred to as 'boys.' For example, a commentator might say about a famous tennis player that she is 'the wonder girl of women's tennis' (Messner et al. 1993: 127). Also, the researchers found that it was much more likely for women to be referred to by their first names compared to men. This is shown in Table 5.5.

As Table 5.5 illustrates, compared with the men, the women tennis players were over six times more likely to be referred to by their first names. What do these findings mean? The authors offer this interpretation:

> The practice of referring more 'formally' to dominants [those in a higher position] and more 'informally' (or 'endearingly') to subordinates linguistically grants the former adult status, while marking the latter in an infantilizing way. And research suggests these linguistic differences both reflect and (re)construct inequality. (1993: 128)

This example of content analysis treats the text from sports commentaries as *both* a reflection of social structures (i.e., gender inequality) and its cause. This research is also a good illustration of the method of content analysis. It shows how researchers move from collecting data, to developing a set of categories, to testing their reliability, and finally to analyzing their findings. Below is a summary of these steps:

1   Theory and circumstances suggest the selection of particular texts.
2   Sample texts if there are too many to analyse completely.
3   Construct a coding frame [categorization scheme] that fits both the theoretical considerations and the materials.
4   Pilot and revise the coding frame and explicitly define the coding rules.
5   Test the reliability of codes, and sensitize coders to ambiguities.
6   Code all materials in the sample, and establish the overall reliability of the process.
8   Set up a data file for the purpose of statistical analysis.
9   Write a codebook including (a) the rationale of the coding frame; (b) the frequency distribution of all codes; and (c) the reliability of the coding process. (Bauer 2000: 149)

As a qualitative approach, content analysis is widely used by researchers. Its potential to transform large segments of descriptive data into quantified categories is embraced by sociologists who are interested in more 'objective' and formulaic methods of data analysis. As a whole, in content analysis, researchers select excerpts from written texts, talk or interviews and transform them into standardized codes. Other methods of analysis might focus more on the context and coherence of people's stories in everyday interactions. In the following section, I look at how qualitative data is interpreted using narrative analysis. I offer a general discussion on the status and definition of narratives in sociological research and highlight two ways of analyzing such data.

Narrative analysis

Narrative has become a buzzword among sociologists in recent years. The general consensus among qualitative researchers is that stories and storytelling are common methods of sharing information. From this perspective, most things you read, hear, or see are storied (be it research reports, novels, everyday conversations, or movies). Thus, the goal of qualitative analysis becomes understanding what stories convey and how.

For some researchers, the narrative form itself is viewed as a 'natural' and 'humanizing' way of speaking about social life:

Narrative displays the goals and intentions of human actors; it makes individuals, cultures, societies, and historical epochs comprehensible as wholes; it humanizes time; and it allows us to contemplate the effects of our actions; and to alter the direction of our lives. Narrative is everywhere; it is present in myth, fable, short story, epic, history, tragedy, comedy, social histories, fairy tales, novels, science schema, comic strips, conversation, and journal articles. (Richardson 1990a: 117)

In contrast, other sociologists, while acknowledging the prevalence of narratives, caution against treating them as unique and preferred modes of communication. For these researchers, narratives should be analyzed and understood like any other form of social science data. In the words of Atkinson:

> The ubiquity of the narrative and its centrality … are not license simply to privilege those forms. It is the work of anthropologists and sociologists to examine those narratives and to subject them to the same analysis as any other forms. We need to pay due attention to their construction in use: how actors improvise their personal narratives.… We need to attend to how socially shared resources of rhetoric and narrative are deployed to generate recognizable, plausible, and culturally well-informed accounts … What we cannot afford to do is to be seduced by the cultural conventions we seek to study. We should not endorse those cultural conventions that seek to privilege the account as a special kind of representation. (1997: 341; see also Atkinson and Silverman 1997)

As evident in these two positions, there is disagreement among sociologists about the status and importance of narratives. Does this mean that we should abandon narrative analysis and look for a more 'solid' framework? Not necessarily — let me explain why. We are sometimes dismayed by debates in which professionals in the same discipline take diametrically opposed positions on the same topic. This gives rise to questions like 'Don't they know what they are doing?' or 'So, what is the *right* way to do this?' While these questions are perfectly legitimate, we should try to balance the need for definitive statements about 'right' or 'wrong' with the realization that in the academic world answers to such questions emerge from continuing debate.

Making tentative statements that are constantly debated by one's peers is one way scientific knowledge is generated (see Popper 1959). So it is not that sociologists 'don't know what they are talking about,' rather, their commitment to scientific inquiry requires that they allow for someone else knowing more than, or differently from, they do. With this in mind, the subsequent discussions are not intended to settle the question about 'the right way' to do narrative analysis (matters of right or wrong are more efficiently settled by religious and legal authorities than by social scientists). Instead, I highlight some basic themes and approaches to whet the beginner's appetite.

Specifically, this section offers:

1   a working definition of the word 'narrative';
2   basic research questions we can ask about narratives; and
3   two styles of narrative analysis (narrative practice and self-presentations in narratives).

What is a narrative and how can it be analyzed?

In *Narrative Analysis* Riessman (1993: 17–18) notes that a narrative can be defined along a number of dimensions. The first of these is sequence, or the order in which a story is told (what comes first in the story, what comes after, and so forth). She suggests most of us expect stories to be narrated in a linear fashion where one event logically follows another, but there are other ways of storytelling. For example, stories could be articulated in relation to spiritual or familial themes. Instead of a linear story from birth to present time, a respondent's autobiography might start with: 'Let me begin by telling you about my family… I come from a very large family. I have five brothers and three sisters…'

For example, in an ethnography of 'street hustlers' (the chronically homeless and poor who live on the streets and support themselves through criminal activities), Fleisher (1995) writes about how he had to modify his interview questions to accommodate the respondents' way of storytelling:

> At first, I tried to collect interviews by using 'cultural' stages that made sense to me, moving from early childhood and preschool to early adolescence and primary school, then to teenage years and middle school, and so on, proceeding through high school. But their memories didn't seem to be organized by this cultural sequence. I switched, instead to an event sequence of interviewing that focused on major turning points; alcohol use and first involvement in crime; parental divorce, gang membership, drug use, and delinquency; first arrest and first commitment; first crime partner. This technique improved the retrieval of life history information. (1995: 63–64)

In addition to the sequence of events, narratives can also be categorized in terms of their genre. For our purposes, genre refers to a particular class or typology of narratives that follow a recognizable way of telling. According to Riessman:

> When we hear stories, for instance, we expect protagonists, inciting conditions, and culminating events. But not all narratives (or all lives) take this form. Some other genres include habitual narratives (when events happen over and over and consequently there is no peak in action), hypothetical narratives (which depict events that did not happen), and topic-centered narratives (snapshots of past events that are linked thematically). (1993: 18)

For example, a typical way of storytelling for former drug addicts is the redemption genre. Their narratives tend to begin with horrid descriptions of how bad things were and end with accounts of miraculous recoveries and prospects for a brighter future. Many of us may recognize this mode of storytelling from public reports about the lives of Hollywood celebrities and rock stars, who reportedly overcame their so-called 'demons' before becoming smashing success stories.

In a broad sociological sense, a narrative could be defined as a way of sharing information with others following a particular pattern of telling (genre and order). In qualitative data analysis, narratives are also explored along a number of other dimensions. For example, according to Cortazzi (2001), narratives could be analyzed based on their:

- content (the substance of the story)
- structure (how the story is told)
- functions (the purposes the story serves)
- context (in what place or setting the story is told).

While these methods of analysis are interrelated, different analysts may choose to emphasize one aspect or another in their work. For example, one researcher might examine narratives in an interpersonal context, whereas another might be interested in their use in organizational or institutional settings.

Cortazzi notes that narrative analysis is not limited to the examination of the respondents' lives, but it can also be applied to understanding the experiences of the researcher. On the one hand, narratives tell us about the meaning of the respondents' lives (i.e., how they interpret their world) and the ways in which they articulate or voice their experiences (i.e., how they tell their stories, from what position, and emphasizing what human qualities). On the other hand, looking at narrative quality from the perspective of the researcher's experiences means turning the focus of the qualitative research on itself. In this context, it is reasonable to pose the same questions about the researcher as the ones directed at the respondents. That means asking: How does the researcher view the world and tell her or his story? Accordingly, the product of a research project, the written report, is a story in its own right (see Atkinson 1992 and Van Maanen 1988 for a detailed discussion of ethnographic writing). This is particularly applicable to ethnographic studies that self-consciously adopt narrative formats to convey their findings. In Cortazzi's words, the ethnographic text could be viewed 'as a narrative account of a quest, discovery and interpretation – the journey from outsider to insider …' (2001: 387).

In the remainder of this section, two approaches to narrative analysis will be presented. The first is Gubrium and Holstein's (1997b) narrative practice approach, which looks at how stories are produced, for what purposes, and under what conditions. We then examine Riessman's (2002) analysis of narratives with its emphasis on how people present themselves in their stories.

Narrative practice: how narratives are put together

According to Gubrium and Holstein (1997b) narrative practice attempts to balance two competing concerns: how a story is told and what it contains. As the authors put it:

> We use the term 'narrative practice' to characterize simultaneously the activities of storytelling, the sources used to tell stories, and the auspices under which stories are told. Considering personal stories and their coherence as matters of practice centers attention on the relation between these 'hows' and 'whats' of narration.... Orienting to practice allows us to see the storytelling process as both actively constructive and locally constrained. (p. 164)

Narrative practice (or what Gubrium and Holstein more generally refer to as 'interpretive practice') aims to simultaneously study *what* people say or do and *how* they make it meaningful. The assumption here is that social life, and narratives in particular, are shaped through a set of practices and conditions that make them meaningful. The analysis aims to show how the artful practice of speaking and the concrete circumstances of social life come together to form social reality. To illustrate this approach and its various concepts, let us consider the example of a job interview.

Jane, a bright college graduate with a degree in business administration, is being interviewed for a job with a large banking firm. The interview is taking place at the company's branch office near her hometown. She enters the building and introduces herself to the receptionist who directs her to the room where she will meet Mr. Johnson, the company's recruiter. After a few uncomfortable moments of waiting, Mr. Johnson enters the interview room. He is a middle-aged white male dressed in a suit. The interview begins shortly thereafter and one of the first questions posed to Jane is, 'Why don't you tell me about yourself?' This presents her with an opportunity to tell a story about herself. She might say:

> Where do I begin? [She chuckles.] Well, I have always been good with counting money – ever since I was a child. My parents bought me a toy cash register when I was ten and I had a lot of fun playing with that…. So when I finished high school and it was time to go to college, I decided business administration was the right career for me. I got very good grades in college, as you can see in my resume, and worked as an intern at The First International Bank during the summer…

Notice that Jane doesn't just tell Mr. Johnson anything that crosses her mind, like how she and her friends went to a 'cool' party the night before and met some very interesting people. The story about last night's party, however interesting it might be to her personally, is of no relevance in this job interview. What Mr. Johnson wants to know is another kind of story altogether, one that highlights job-related skills and Jane's overall ability to communicate and get along with others. In this context, the substance of the story, *how* it is told, and *where* are all interrelated parts of the social construction of Jane's identity as a 'good employee.' In analyzing this example, the question that narrative practice asks is: How does Jane construct a good-employee story that reflects both her biography and suits the needs of the occasion? To answer this question, we can make use of two concepts put forth by Gubrium and Holstein: 'narrative composition' and 'narrative control.'

Narrative composition has to do with how a story is told or how it is made coherent and meaningful. In Jane's job interview, note how she narratively links her childhood interests with a career in business administration. This is what Gubrium and Holstein would call a 'narrative linkage' or a descriptive connection that maintains the flow of a story. As descriptive devices, Jane's linkages encourage Mr. Johnson to see her as someone who is 'naturally' suited for the job.

A related dimension of Jane's narrative composition is her 'footing' or the point of view from which the story is told. Notice how her story has a biographical nature. It highlights a natural progression from childhood to her present desire to be involved in banking. Jane's narrative footing for this interview is summarized by the statement, 'I was born to do this job.' However, this is not the only possible footing from which a candidate could present herself. For example, Jane could have started with:

To be honest with you, Mr. Johnson, I just graduated from college and need money to pay off my debts. So I'll take any job and work any hours you want me to... I am two months behind with rent and if I could have an advance for this job, it would be a big help – if that's not being too pushy.

The above narrative footing presents Jane's interest in the job in an entirely different light. Her financial needs, rather than her natural skills, are the basis of her request for the job.

With 'narrative control,' the focus is more on the contextual factors that direct the flow and content of the story. Jane is telling her story in a particular setting. There are certain expectations at work here. For example, she knows that her story is being evaluated by Mr. Johnson and the outcome of his decision could result in her gainful employment. The conditions of the setting are not incidental aspects of the narrative; rather, they directly control the substance of the presentation. Had Jane met Mr. Johnson at a single's bar, for example, and was asked the question, 'Why don't you tell me about yourself?' her response would have been very different. Indeed, she might have opted not to respond altogether, or tell Mr. Johnson to 'buzz off.'

Similarly, if the question were posed to Jane during a psychotherapy session, the unfolding narrative would delve into personal issues such as childhood, intimate relationships, family, and so on. In fact, as a patient in therapy her reluctance to speak in these terms could be interpreted as a manifestation of her mental dysfunction (e.g., 'fear of intimacy' or 'inability to be emotionally expressive'). In analyzing narratives, attention to the setting could help us understand the implicit and explicit controls that shape how people tell their stories. In the example of the job interview, narrative control means that the focus of the interaction would be on work-related skills and signs of good moral character. In a sense, the practical goal of a job interview (i.e., its narrative task) is to evaluate employability based on a formulaic question-response format.

We can also think of narrative control in relation to how stories are 'monitored' or 'edited.' In most social settings, either the storytellers themselves or their intended audience edit or intervene in the narrative to make it more coherent or relevant for the occasion. This is especially evident in organizational settings where clients are often warned to get their stories straight or suffer the consequences. The following is an example of narrative editing as practiced by a social worker during a screening interview at a homeless shelter. The goal of a screening interview is to assess clients' needs and to inform them about shelter policies. The typical story on such occasions is about the dire circumstances (e.g., poverty and poor health) that led to the client being homeless. In this extract, notice how when the homeless client fails to present a relevant story for the occasion, the social worker confronts him to edit his narrative:

Social worker: All right. Can you think of anything else?
Tim: I think that's probably got it.
Social worker: Okay.

Tim: That's got me fixed up. Not unless you got any million-dollar checks?
Social worker: Um, let me check my drawers here. [They both laugh.]
Tim: Okay, remember when we were talking about, you know, what was it, World War, World War I and II veterans? [They were] supposed to have some allies in Burma, you know. Uh, Burma, and Algiers, all different kinds of places, you know, where they, and they – you know, army people, military people are funny, you know, about money. Where it's at, who gets it and everything, you know. Who's acceptable, you know. They may not like someone because he may be a toughie. May not be any good. They say, 'No, you ain't gonna get, no money. We don't like you.' And so you'll never get no money…
Social worker: So what are you saying? You didn't get your money when you got out of the service?
Tim: No. Uh, I didn't get no million if I supposed to get one. I didn't get one …
Social worker: Well, think about it, Tim. If they gave you a million dollars when you got discharged from the service, then everyone would join the service.
Tim: Right, uh-huh.
Social worker: And they're not, so I don't – there may be some kind of separation pay. But it's not as much as a million bucks.
Tim: Uh-huh. [Pause] Well, that should do me, hon.
Social worker: Okay.
Tim: Thanks much.
Social worker: Okay. Well, as long as you keep cooperating and so forth while you're here, we'll have you through the weekend.
Tim: Okay. I thank you so much, dear. (Adapted from Marvasti 2002: 643–45)

The client's fanciful line of inquiry about a 'million–dollar check' is of no organizational relevance, so he is not allowed to go on. At first, the social worker gives him the chance to get back on track, so to speak, but his refusal to be coherent, at least in locally relevant terms, causes the social worker to become more direct in her attempts to monitor the unfolding narrative until eventually she stops the story altogether.

Therefore, the concept of narrative practice with its dual emphasis on composition and control provides an analytical framework that moves beyond the search for authenticity or truth in storytelling. Instead of asking whether stories are real or not, narrative practice looks at what purposes they serve under what conditions. The next section offers a slightly different view of narrative analysis.

Self-presentation in narratives

Riessman (2002) takes a somewhat different approach to analyzing narratives. She asks: How do people present themselves in their personal stories? Borrowing from Goffman's work (1959) on self-presentation in everyday life (i.e., dramaturgy), Riessman argues that interview narratives could be treated as descriptive performances:

> As Goffman (1959, 1981) suggests … social actors stage performances of desirable selves. … To emphasize the performative elements is not to suggest identities are inauthentic, but only that they are situated and accomplished in interaction.
>
> Applying these insights to interviews, informants [respondents] negotiate how they want to be known by the stories they develop collaboratively with their audiences. Informants do not reveal an essential self as much as they perform a preferred one, selected from the multiplicity of selves that individuals switch among as they go about their lives. (2002: 701)

Riessman, like Gubrium and Holstein (1997b), is interested in *how* narratives create meaning for a particular purpose or audience. She shows how narrators, especially women, construct their identities in their stories. Riessman's analysis emphasizes what she terms 'social positioning' or 'how narrators choose to position audiences, characters, and themselves' (2002: 701). In the example below, using excerpts from an interview with an Asian woman, Riessman shows the changes in social positionings as the story unfolds. After hinting at the circumstances of her first failed pregnancy, the respondent, Gita, goes on to describe how she had to go against the advice of her doctor:

> Because I already told you   Scene 3
> it was during that period that [name] the socialist leader
> led the gigantic procession against Mrs. Indira Gandhi,
> the Prime Minister of India, in Delhi.
> And I was a political leader [names place and party]
> I had to participate in that.
> So I went by train to Delhi
> but returned by plane.
> After the return I was in [name] Nursing Home
> for 16 days bleeding.
> And so he [husband] was very angry   Scene 4
> he said 'do not go for any social work
> do not be active' this and that.
> But afterwards I never became– [pregnant] (Riessman 2002: 700)

According to Riessman, from 'Scene 3' to 'Scene 4' Gita's social positioning changes from a political activist to a wife. This shift in self-presentation communicates the complexities of the respondent's life and the conflicting social conditions that shaped her identity: Gita had to balance family responsibilities with the demands of being a political leader.

Riessman states that narrative analysis in general helps researchers preserve the integrity, complexity, and the full meaning of respondents' personal narratives:

> Narratives are a particularly significant genre for representing and analyzing identity in its multiple guises in different contexts. The methods allow for the systematic study of

experience and, for feminist researchers such as myself, the changing meanings of conditions that affect women disproportionately, including domestic violence, reproductive illness, and poverty. (2002: 707)

For Riessman, the strength of narrative analysis lies in its ability to look at qualitative data, particularly information from in-depth interviews, in its full social context. Whereas some forms of qualitative analysis (e.g., content analysis) break people's statements into quantifiable chunks at the researcher's discretion, narrative analysis aims to fully understand how various pieces of data relate to one another under the demands of the setting in which they are articulated.

Another type of qualitative analysis that examines the particulars of everyday life is conversation analysis, whose goal is to reveal how social reality is produced through talk. I introduce some of the basic themes of this approach and offer how-to advice using discussions and examples from Silverman's *Interpreting Qualitative Data: Methods for Analyzing Talk, Text and Interaction* (2001).

Conversation Analysis

Conversation analysis (CA) makes everyday talk the topic of investigation. It is influenced by a branch of sociology known as ethnomethodology, or the study of how people in the course of their everyday activities achieve social reality and order. Note that ethnomethodology views reality as something that is 'accomplished' through social interaction (Garfinkel 1967); reality is not inherently meaningful but it becomes meaningful through what people say and/or do. CA follows ethnomethodology's project by investigating how everyday conversations produce social reality; it empirically shows, with as much detail as possible, *how* social reality is brought to life through verbal exchanges and their taken for granted norms. As Silverman states, 'Conversation analysis is based on an attempt to describe people's methods for producing orderly interaction [through talk]' (2001: 167).

The term 'talk' has important theoretical connotations for conversation analysts. It implies a distinction between 'naturally occurring' and 'researcher-provoked' data (Silverman 2001: 159). Researcher-provoked data refers to what people say in response to specific research questions, especially during interviews. By contrast, the term 'naturally occurring talk' is used to capture what people say in everyday situations, such as home, work, television talk shows, news programs, or schools.

Silverman acknowledges that the distinction has its limitations. Particularly, the word 'natural' should not be taken to mean pristine or untouched. All data, be it research interviews or talk, involve human interaction and interpretive activity. However, there are contextual differences between what people say in an interview versus an ordinary conversation. We do interviews with the hope of understanding how people do things in their 'natural' interactions with others – when the researcher is not present at the scene. As Silverman states:

if we do not push it too far, it can still be helpful to make use of the distinction between two kinds of data: naturally occurring and researcher-provoked. Indeed, if we can, at least to some extent, study what people are actually doing in 'naturally occurring' situations, why should we ever want to work with 'researcher-provoked' data? (2001: 159)

If talk is not superior to interviews, it is at least an equally important source of information for the study of human interaction.

When analyzing everyday talk, conversation analysts are particularly interested in what Sacks called 'membership categorization devices,' or a particular set of descriptions 'plus their rules of application' (1972: 332, cited in Silverman 2001: 141). Conversation analysts want to know how we use special categories like 'mother' or 'child' in everyday talk. For example, Silverman (2001: 130) points out that in the sentence 'The X cried. The Y picked it up,' most people assume that X is the child and Y is the mother. CA asks why we make such an assumption, based on what rules. Why is it, for example, that it is far less likely for us to assume X is an abandoned baby and Y is a street tramp? Or for that matter, X could conceivably be a rabid dog and Y the veterinarian who has to euthanize the poor animal. As Baker (1997: 143) puts it, membership categorization devices are 'the speakers' 'puppets', which they dress up in different ways and make behave in various ways…'. Research on how people create and apply these descriptive categories helps us better understand how society is organized.

To empirically investigate the use of descriptive resources in naturally occurring talk, conversation analysts create detailed transcriptions. CA transcripts of talk follow specific guidelines for capturing every aspect of a conversation (overlaps, pauses, intonations, and so on). Below is an example of a CA transcript followed by Table 5.6 which gives an abbreviated transcription guide:

> (S's wife has just slipped a disc)
>
> 1 **H:** And we were wondering if there's *anything* we can do to help
> 2 **S:** [Well 'at's
> 3 **H:** [I mean can we do any shopping for her something like tha:t?
> 4   (.07)
> 5 **S:** Well that's *most* ki:nd Heather*ton* .hhh At the moment
> 6   no: because we've still got two bo:ys at home (Silverman
>   2001: 164)

While at first glance the level of specificity might seem awkward, it is important to keep in mind that for CA researchers it is the details of conversation that show 'the artful use of talk' (Baker 1997: 131). Also, the meticulous investigation of features of talk is a way of ensuring empirical validity, or making sure that you don't speak for your respondents (i.e., you don't put words in their mouths, so to speak). CA's commitment to the empirical is captured in the following statements by Heritage:

TABLE 5.6   *Abbreviated transcription symbols*

[	Left brackets indicate the point at which a current speaker's talk is overlapped by another's talk
‘	Indicates a continuing intonations
(.07)	Numbers in parentheses indicate elapsed time in silence in tenths of seconds
::	Colons indicate the prolongation of the immediately prior sound. The length of the row of colons indicates the length of the prolongation
.hhh	A row of h's prefixed by a dot indicates an inbreath; without a dot, an outbreath. The length of row of h's indicates the length of the inbreath or outbreath

Source: Adapted from Silverman 2001: 303

analysis is strongly 'data-driven' – developed from phenomena which are in various ways evidenced in the data of interaction. Correspondingly, there is a strong bias against *a priori* [made before examination] speculation about the orientations and motives of speakers and in favour of detailed examination of conversationalists' actual actions. Thus the empirical conduct of speakers is treated as the central source out of which the analysis may develop. (1984: 243, as cited in Silverman 2001: 167)

The logic behind thorough transcriptions is that the analysis must directly correspond to the data: the greater the level of detail, the tighter the connection between the things people say and how researchers interpret them. The next section presents the basic concepts and examples of CA research.

Interactional sequence

Interactional sequence is the study of how one utterance begets another as the meaning of the reality at hand is negotiated. For example, Heath (1989) shows how the experience of pain and suffering is negotiated in the conversational give-and-take between doctors and their patients. He observes that patients, through their utterances, facial expressions, and body movements, construct and manage the experience of physical pain in interaction with their physicians. In the following extract, a patient is being evaluated for an aching foot. Notice how 'pain' is negotiated through the patient's responses to the physician's questions and manipulation of the injured foot.

(Dr. = Doctor, P = Patient)

Dr. You've got some varicose veins haven't you (.)
Dr. eh bit (2.3)
P   arghhh*hhh(*hm)
Dr. is that sore when I do [that? mhm hhum (.5)
P   he:ragh:

Dr.   *um (2.5)
Dr.   *hhh (.) just stand up (.) Missus Delft (.) will you

(Adapted from Heath 1989: 115)

Here, pain (a natural response to discomfort) is socially achieved through the interaction with the physician. The patient becomes a neutral observer to her or his own malady as the doctor manipulates the injured body part. In this CA study, instead of taking the notion of 'pain' for granted as an objective medical reality, Heath shows us how the experience of physical suffering is socially accomplished through the doctor-patient interactions. In other words, pain is not external to the interaction, but it is understood through it.

An important aspect of the interactional sequence for CA researchers is 'turn-taking,' which refers to the expectations that are invoked when one person speaks and another listens. According to Silverman, this seemingly simple feature of talk involves a complex set of understandings and implicit agreements. For example, turn-taking creates demands for listening to the speaker. In Silverman's words:

> The turn-taking system provides an 'intrinsic motivation' for listening to all utterances in a conversation. Interest or politeness alone is not sufficient to explain such attention. Rather, every participant must listen to and analyse each utterance in case(s) he is selected as the next speaker. (2001: 168)

The concept of turn-taking could be applied to understanding student-teacher interactions in the classroom. For example, consider what happens when an instructor uses the discussion format instead of lecturing. Given CA's understanding of turn-taking, we might expect students to become more attentive. This is because the discussion format requires that they be prepared to fulfill their turn in the conversation by saying something meaningful; otherwise, they might suffer embarrassment or appear less than intelligent.

Institutional interaction

For conversation analysts, institutional interaction refers to the relationship between institutional context and talk. It is worth noting that here the word 'context' does not refer to a concrete setting or place. CA rejects the so called 'bucket' theory (Heritage 1997: 163), which views 'context' as a sort of external container that bounds social interaction. Instead, the substance of institutional context from a CA perspective is assumed to be embedded in the talk or social interaction itself. As Heritage states:

> The assumption is that it is fundamentally through interaction that context is built, invoked and managed, and that it is through interaction that institutional imperatives originating from outside the interaction are evidenced and made real and enforceable for participants. We want to find out how that works. Empirically, this means showing that the participants build context of their talk in and through their talk. (1997: 163)

Therefore, when doing CA research, we should not separate the context from the talk itself. Any reference to institutional context should be based on empirical data. For example, let us say that in your analysis of prison inmates' conversations, you come across the following transcript:

Inmate one: Hey, why don't you get the hell out of my way!
Inmate two: Yeah! Why don't you make me?

From a CA perspective, you cannot conclude about this exchange that the oppressive environment of the prison forces these inmates to be verbally abusive to one another. The connection between the 'oppressive environment' and 'abusive language' cannot be made unless it is empirically evident in the data. To make an empirical case for how the institutional context of prison affects the inmate's lives you need a statement like, 'Man, this place's like hell. It robs you of your dignity. It turns you into an animal. If you don't fight and yell back, you're dead.'

Given this understanding of institutional context, let us now consider a CA study of how the context of objective reporting or neutrality is achieved in the TV news. In this research, Clayman (1992, as discussed in Silverman 2001: 172–73) argues that when asking controversial questions, TV interviewers create a sense of neutrality by changing their 'footing,' or the perspective from which they ask the questions. In the following excerpt from Clayman's research, the interviewer from *Meet the Press* (a weekly U.S. news program in which prominent politicians are interviewed about current events) shifts his footing as he makes a controversial statement about the former U.S. president, Ronald Reagan:

(IV = interviewer)

1 **IV**: Senator, (.05) uh: *President* Reagan's elected thirteen months
          ago: an
2   en*or*mous landslide.
3   (.08)
4 **IV**: It is s::*aid* that his *programs* are in trouble

(Clayman 1992, as cited in Silverman 2001: 172)

The interviewer shifts from a firm declaration in his initial remark in lines 1–2 to the tentative passive tense ('It is said') in line 4. According to Clayman, the change in footing helps attribute the statement to a third party (i.e., 'Someone out there said this, not I, but could you answer it anyway?'). In most cases, the interviewee plays his or her part by tacitly accepting the rules of the conversation. It is highly unlikely for the senator to respond with, '*It* was said by *whom*? I think this is just your opinion.' As seen in this study, CA studies try to show how the rules of the setting, or the institutional context, are sustained through talk.

TABLE 5.7   *How to do CA*

1	Always try to identify sequences of talk.
2	Try to examine how speakers take on certain roles or identities through their talk (e.g. questioner-answerer or client-professional).
3	Look for particular outcomes in the talk (e.g. a request for clarification, a repair, laughter) and work backward to trace the trajectory through which a particular outcome was produced.

Source: Silverman 2001: 177

TABLE 5.8   *Common errors to avoid when doing CA*

1	Explaining a turn at talk by reference to the speaker's intentions.
2	Explaining a turn at talk by reference to a speaker's role or status (e.g. as a doctor or as a man or woman).
3	Trying to make sense of a single line of transcript or utterance in isolation from the surrounding talk.

Source: Silverman 2001: 177

Tables 5.7 and 5.8 highlight Silverman's advice for CA researchers and the common errors they should avoid.

To summarize, through detailed empirical analysis of every day talk in various settings CA shows how social reality and order are achieved and maintained. Next we examine discourse analysis (DA), the last type of qualitative data analysis presented in this chapter. The following section describes the basic features of this approach and discusses two of its variants (interactional and Foucauldian) along with examples.

Discourse analysis

Discourse analysis (DA) has been defined and used across many disciplines (e.g., sociology, psychology, communications, linguistics, education, etc.). According to Gill, there are at least fifty-seven different ways of doing DA:

> The terms 'discourse' and 'discourse analysis' are highly contested. To claim that one's approach is a discourse analytical one does not necessarily tell anybody much; it is not a simple definitional issue, but involves taking up a position in an extremely charged – though important – set of arguments. (2000: 173)

Therefore, it is difficult to define DA as a unified body of research and theory; it has different meanings and applications for researchers from a wide range of disciplines. Nonetheless, Gill lists a number of central themes in DA that are shared by researchers in this area. Among these are:

* viewing discourse and language as being productive of social reality (discourse doesn't simply describe reality but it creates it as well)

- treating discourse as a type of social action in its own right (discourse is not just a description but it does things)
- emphasizing the rhetorical functions of discourse (discourse is to promote one side of a conflict). (2000: 174–76)

Taken together, these themes also point to a tentative definition of the word 'discourse.' Specifically, discourse can be defined as a way of writing or speaking that constructs a particular type of knowledge with practical and rhetorical implications. To illustrate this point, consider the following excerpt from Gray's *Men, Women, and Relationships*.

> When a man is attracted to a woman, at some point he will resist his partner and may then seek to change her or deny himself in order to find relief. There are, of course, other ways to obtain relief, like moving from one partner to another, having secret affairs, or developing any addiction that can numb the growing pains of resistance. In any case, to whatever degree he is resisting the emergence of the very qualities he was attracted to, he will seek to avoid true relating. (1993: 71)

What do you hear in this passage? In particular, what way of knowing is invoked about male–female relationships? The discourse of gender articulated here assumes that there are essential differences between male and female worldviews, the former is presented as being psychologically less developed. Remember that we defined discourse as being constructive, active, and rhetorical. In this example, (a) the author discursively *constructs* men as having difficulty establishing meaningful relationships; (b) the description is *active* in that it suggests men's problems lead them to behave differently (e.g., have affairs); and (c) in a *rhetorical* sense, the emphasis on essential gender differences implies that compared to women, men are less capable of 'true relating.'

Given these general statements about the meaning and application of discourse analysis, let us now look at two applications of this approach.

Interactional discourse analysis

What is loosely labeled interactional discourse analysis here is similar to CA, or conversation analysis, insofar as it is concerned with how social reality is accomplished through everyday talk (for a discussion of some of the differences between the two approaches see Silverman 2001: 188–89). According to Silverman (p. 178), this type of analysis begins with the assumption that language is a kin to social action. Influenced by the works of the British philosopher J. L. Austin (1962), interactional DA examines how our spoken words make us accountable to others. As Silverman notes, when you scream, 'Help!,' you have done something; you have committed yourself and would-be rescuers to cooperative action toward your relief. Conceptualizing language in this way, interactional DA aims to empirically demonstrate how discourses accomplish reality in everyday talk.

Among the many analytical tools used by interactional discourse analysts is the concept of 'interpretive repertoire' (Potter 1996; Silverman 2001: 179–82). This concept is used in roughly the same manner as the word discourse, which we defined as a way of knowing and speaking that constructs a particular version of reality. However, compared to the broadly defined notion of discourse, interpretive repertoires are based on more systematic and locally circumscribed (specific) usages. Silverman's study of 'motherhood as repertoire' (2001: 180–82) is an interesting case in point, which shows how motherhood is descriptively constructed in talk. In the extract below, the mother of a diabetic sixteen-year-old is talking with her daughter's physician:

(D = doctor; M = mother of June, aged 16)

1 **M:** She's going through a very languid stage ( ) she won't do anything unless
2 you'd push her
3 **D:** so you're finding you're having to push her quite a lot?
4 **M:** mm no well I don't (.) I just leave her now (Adapted from Silverman 2001: 181)

Silverman argues that in the above passage motherhood is constructed through the theme of 'young adult's autonomy' (i.e., 'I am a good mother because I respect my child's independence.'). The mother uses the interpretive repertoire of respecting the independence of young people to defend herself against the accusatory question, 'so you're finding you're having to push her quite a lot?' The reality project of this exchange is to convince the doctor that she is not a 'pushy' mother. But notice how later during the same consultation a different understanding of motherhood emerges:

1 **M:** I don't think she's really sticking to her diet (.) I don't know the effects
2 this will have on her (.) it's bound to alter her sugar if she's not got the
3 right insulin isn't it? I mean I know what she eats at home but [outside
4 **D:** [so there's no real consistency to her diet? It's sort
5 [of
6 **M:** [no well I keep it as consistent as I can at home (Adapted from Silverman 2001: 181)

In the second extract, the charge of being too lenient as implied by 'so there's no real consistency' is countered by the statement about being consistent at home, which in turn helps construct motherhood as 'parental responsibility' (i.e., 'I am a good mother because I control my child.').

In this study, there are two systems of interpretation, or two ways of knowing motherhood that in some ways contradict each other. Accordingly to

Silverman, the two opposing images of motherhood ('parental responsibility' versus 'respecting young adult's autonomy') could coexist because they are discursive resources that are artfully used to achieve the interpretive tasks of showing that the mother of this diabetic patient is neither irresponsible nor pushy.

In addition to interpretive repertoires, interactional DA makes use of many other concepts (see Silverman 2001: 183–88 for a description of a number of other concepts such as 'stakes' and 'scripts.'). As stated earlier, DA is not limited to one particular approach. In the next section, I present a style of DA that could be applied to the analysis of social institutions and written texts.

Foucauldian discourse analysis

Foucault, a renowned social scientist/historian/philosopher, applied the concept of discourse to the analysis of representations of knowledge as found in historical documents. Of particular interest to him was the relationship between power and knowledge (Foucault 1980). He argued that the modern era is founded on the belief that the application of reason and science is an inherently humane method of promoting social progress. However, he claimed that modernity fails to recognize that whenever knowledge of any form is applied, it accompanies the exercise of power. For example, when we solicit the knowledge and expertise of psychotherapists, we are in a sense submitting to their authority and power, especially when we invite them to define our identities through various therapeutic means.

To underscore the reflexive (give-and-take) relationship between power and knowledge, Foucault analyzed historical documents to show how the exercise of power and ways of knowing dramatically change over time, and not always for the better. A distinct premise of his analysis was that the subject (i.e., the person whose intentions and thoughts are supposedly the source of knowledge) is itself a social construct. In his words, 'One has to dispense with the constituent subject, and get rid of the subject itself, that's to say, to arrive at an analysis which can account for the constitution of the subject within a historical framework' (Foucault 1980: 117, as cited in Best and Kellner 1991: 51).

Thus much of his research was devoted to showing how the subject, or the self, is constructed through the various discourses of psychiatry, medicine, and crime. According to Foucault, such discourses produce certain ways of understanding who we should be and what we should do. These self-imposed mandates are in essence the exercise of power through knowledge. For example, in *Discipline and Punish* (1977) Foucault underscores the historical origins of the modern criminal justice system. Specifically, he argues that the modern methods of treating criminals are no more humane than the barbaric practices of the past (i.e., torture); rather, they are simply more effective means of social control. Foucault supports this position by the observation that, modern criminal justice produces subjects who willingly keep *themselves* under surveillance (i.e., citizens who police themselves). While the criminal justice authorities no longer use cruel forms of punishment (e.g., flogging or public hangings), their power of control has not diminished.

Institutional discourse analysis applies Foucault's work to the study of how and for what practical purposes subjects or selves are constructed within institutional settings (see Gubrium and Holstein 2001). Among other questions, this approach asks what discursive resources enable institutional agents (e.g., psychiatrists, welfare workers, police officers, etc.) to practice authority or power over their clients, and in turn, how do the clients counteract these measures by using discursive resources of their own? (See for example, Miller and Holstein 1995 and Spencer 2001.)

These kinds of analyses are similar to what was discussed in the previous section concerning interpretive repertoires. The analysis of discourse in sociology at an institutional level also tends to focus on how locally defined and systematically applied ways of knowing help construct the realities of the occasion and accomplish the tasks at hand. The difference in part has to do with how 'institutional context' is defined. In interactional DA, the context is viewed as something that is itself constructed through talk. Foucauldian discourse analysis, at least as applied in sociological circles, tends to approach institutional context as more or less a given material reality within which interpretive work is done.

For example, in a study of a 'welfare-to-work program' (a program designed to help the recipients of government assistance overcome poverty and obtain full-time employment), Miller and Holstein look at 'how organizational settings furnish the conditions of possibility for reality construction and reality contests…' (1995: 37). In particular, the authors look at how the program participants and the staff create and resolve disputes using a range of discursive resources within particular organizational boundaries. In this type of analysis, discourses are available resources (like the ingredients in a kitchen pantry); what meals people prepare with them depends on the specifics of the situation and the individual participants involved.

Another approach to studying discourse, textual discourse analysis, applies Foucault's concepts to the study of written texts. When used with this kind of data, as Prior (1997) notes, Foucaudian DA focuses on 'authority' of the text (the social and political factors that give a written work the power to influence human action) rather than its 'authorship' (who wrote it). So the focus is not the presumed subject behind the text and her or his intentions but what realities or ways of seeing are made possible through the text. For example, in an intriguing analysis of a World Health Organization (1997) report about causes of death, Prior points out that the report's classification system is more reflective of certain ideological beliefs about social order than particular facts about how people die. Table 5.9 lists the causes of death according to the World Health Organization as presented in Prior's research.

Prior notes that what is striking about this medically oriented way of seeing death is that social causes, such as poverty, are absent from the categories. For example, when we look at the category of 'complications of pregnancy and

TABLE 5.9   *An abbreviated list of causes of death based on a 1997*
World Health Organization report

Nosological categories (medical classifications of death)
Infectious and parasitic diseases
Neoplasm (tumor)
Endocrine, nutritional and metabolic diseases and immunity disorders
Diseases of the blood and blood forming organs
Mental disorders
Diseases of the nervous system and sense organs
Diseases of the circulatory system
Diseases of the respiratory system
Diseases of the digestive system
Diseases of the genitourinary (genital and urinary organs) system
Complications of pregnancy and childbirth
Diseases of the skin and subcutaneous tissue
Diseases of the musculoskeletal (muscles and skeleton) system and connective tissue
Congenital abnormalities
Conditions originating in the perinatal period
Symptoms, signs and ill-defined conditions
External causes of injury and poisoning

Source: Adapted from Prior 1997: 68

childbirth,' not only is poverty absent but so is its feminization, or how it disproportionately affects women and their health. In a discursive sense, the reader of this report is invited to view the world and its problems from a medical gaze that reduces social conditions to only the diseases of the body. In Prior's words:

> It is, of course, interesting to know that causes of death can be classified at all when one considers the myriad things that can precede a death. It is even more interesting to consider what can and what cannot be regarded as a relevant cause of human fatality. Thus we can see at once, for example, how the vision of death expressed herein is, in the main, one predicated on the human body, its biological subsystems and the diseases to which they fall prey. There is thus no reference to ill-luck, malfeasance or misfortune, nor to more mundane ideas such as poverty or old age or exhaustion... (1997: 67)

For our purposes, this means when we analyze the written text with an eye towards its discursive content, we should not treat the information communicated through the text as rhetorically neutral or a mere statement of the facts. From a Foucauldian DA perspective, all forms of representation involve the dual relationship between power and knowledge, between ways of knowing and their political implications.

To recap, in this section we reviewed two ways of doing discourse analysis: one focused on how discourses are used in talk and one that follows Foucault's emphasis on the power/knowledge relationship as found in institutional practices and in written texts. The following discussion considers the issue of how research findings can be evaluated.

Evaluating findings

We have spent the better part of this chapter going over the different ways qualitative data can be interpreted. I repeatedly stated that the type of analysis you choose depends on your theory, the kind of data you have, and your research questions. But how do we know if the findings accurately reflect what we observed? In other words, how do we evaluate findings from a qualitative research? Below is a brief discussion of a number of concepts and procedures that are used by sociologists to this end.

Validity

Let's say you are having a conversation with a classmate named Joe while waiting for your next class. Joe goes on and on about his family's wealth and social status. He tells you about a vacation the whole family took on the French Riviera last summer, and how they all enjoyed gambling there. However, you have doubts about the veracity of Joe's statements because he wears inexpensive clothes, and as far as you know, he doesn't drive a fancy car or possess other markers of wealth. Overall, the empirical evidence, as you know it, doesn't support his claims of affluence. So you decide Joe is a liar, but how do you know you have judged him accurately, or given him the right label? The issue here is the *validity* of your finding, or the extent to which your assessment of Joe being a liar corresponds to the empirical (observable) reality about him. After all, it is very unfair to make unfounded accusations about people.

In qualitative research, the question of validity is no less important than it is in everyday life. Sociologists throughout the world produce endless volumes of information, offering useful insights about a topic no less ambitious than society itself. Criteria for asking questions and critiquing findings from research are necessary for readers and sociologists alike to navigate their way through this sea of knowledge, to tell the good from the bad, or at least, to make some intelligent choices about what kind of science they want to consume. Thus social scientists can no more dismiss questions of validity than any of us in our everyday lives could refuse to be accountable for our claims about someone being a liar, for example.

What exactly does validity mean to social scientists? Hammersley offers the following definition: 'By validity, I mean truth: interpreted as the extent to which an account accurately represents the social phenomena to which it refers' (1990: 57, as cited in Silverman 2001: 232). To put it another way, validity is about knowing if we called things by their right name based on the available empirical data (Peräkylä 1997). How does one go about testing the validity of qualitative research? The following paragraphs offer three ways of addressing this issue.

One way of testing validity is through respondent validation, which involves taking the research report back to the subjects and asking them questions like:

'What do you think? Do you agree or disagree with my conclusions?' If your respondents think you completely mischaracterized their experiences, then your research lacks validity. However, there are at least three problems with respondent validation (Silverman 2001: 236). First, we cannot assume the respondents have the analytical vocabulary to make sense of sociological writing. Statements like 'in everyday life discourse is both constructive of, and constructed through, members' practices' might mean very little to them. Second, respondents may not be interested in reading our analysis. In fact, my homeless respondents often asked me if I had a 'real job,' or when I was going to get one, thus signaling their appreciation of my research as a hobby and not something substantial like gainful employment. Third, respondent validation will most likely generate antagonism or disapproval if your analysis challenges people's idealized images of themselves.

For example, in my fieldwork at a homeless shelter, the staff saw themselves as pious and caring. Their offices were decorated with religious imagery and drawings of winged angels. My analysis, on the other hand, pointed to the arbitrary and sometimes brutal exercise of power at this site. Many people were denied food and shelter because they had an 'attitude problem' and were deemed 'treatment resistant.' I did not try respondent validation at my research site, but the reaction is predictable. These criticisms are not intended to devalue completely respondent validation, but to suggest that it is not a magic bullet and should be used wisely.

Another strategy for testing validity is triangulation. With this approach the goal is to increase the validity of your findings by collecting data from multiple perspectives (Denzin 1970). For example, a researcher might examine how a welfare agency operates by examining the perspectives of the clients and the staff. However, as with respondent validation, a few words of caution are in order. As Hammersley and Atkinson point out, 'one should not adopt a naively "optimistic" view that the aggregation of data from different sources will unproblematically add up to produce a more complete picture' (1983: 199, as cited in Silverman 2001: 235). Piecing several perspectives together does not mean that at the end the errors cancel each other out to produce a net effect of 'Truth.' A more theoretically enlightened approach to triangulation is to see it as a way of adding complexity and depth to the data and analysis. In this way, social phenomena are approached as multi-sited narratives, each narrator's account is worthy of analysis in its own right.

The last validity check explored in this section involves 'actively seeking out and addressing deviant cases' (Silverman 2001: 239). By deviant cases, I do not mean wayward individuals or social outcasts in our study sample. Deviant cases are those instances of data that do not fit the rest of your analytic model. Deviant case analysis is the 'detailed examination of cases that seem to go against the pattern identified. This may serve to disconfirm the pattern identified, or it may help to add greater sophistication to the analysis' (Gill 2000: 187). This kind of validity check is most useful to qualitative researchers who code their data extensively (e.g., content analysis or grounded theory). These analysts have to explain why some cases do not fit their coding scheme. In fact, when a particular piece of data is incongruent with the rest, that may be a finding worth investigating in itself. In short, deviant case analysis encourages researchers to carefully examine their concepts in relation to all of the data, and not just the parts that 'sound really good.'

Reliability

Another dimension of evaluating research findings is reliability. To go back to our example of the supposed lying classmate, Joe, if we could get a number of students to agree that Joe is indeed a liar, we have achieved reliability of a sort. That is, we have shown that our assessment is recognized and agreed upon by others. Another name for this approach to the problem is 'intercoder reliability,' which means asking other observers to review your analysis and see if they agree with your conclusions. Intercoder reliability is similar to triangulation, in that the use of multiple perspectives is expected to reduce the possibility of misreading the data (i.e., two or more heads are better than one). Another way of thinking about reliability with our imaginary friend, Joe, is to see if when speaking with him some time after you initially labeled him a liar, you still find your characterization of him to be true. This is referred to as 'test–retest reliability.' As a whole, reliability allows us to replicate research results over time and across different investigators or investigations.

The final part of this chapter considers the use of computer software in qualitative data analysis.

Using software in qualitative analysis

As we advance into the computer age, a debate is growing among qualitative researchers about whether computer programs should be used for organizing and analyzing data. In a practical sense, the matter is a forgone conclusion. Computers have already taken over. Most, if not all, qualitative researchers use computers to type, save, and analyze field notes or interview data. Additionally, basic word-processors allow you to search for particular occurrences of a word and move your text through copying and pasting. So, in a subtle and unceremonious way, computers have already crept into qualitative analysis and writing.

Perhaps the question is not 'if' or 'when' but 'how much?' At polar ends of this debate are the 'technophobes' (those who are irrationally fearful of technology) and 'techno philes' (those who are uncritically supportive of all technological advances). Somewhere in the middle are the average consumers who want to weigh the pros and cons before making a purchase and changing the way they do their research and analysis. For these researchers, Weitzman's 'Software and Qualitative Research' (2000) offers some insightful suggestions. Below is a summary of some the key points from this work (for a similar review see also Seale 2000).

Weitzman notes that in the debate about the use of computer software programs in qualitative research there are fears and there are hopes. The fears are that computer programs will take over the analysis; and that novice researchers will adopt the attitude of 'dumping their text into a program and seeing what comes out' (2000: 806). Weitzman dismisses these fears as being based on unlikely scenarios of actual research practice, but he admits that some real problems remain unresolved with the use of computers in qualitative data analysis. One such problem is that software programs are written by analysts with particular backgrounds and interests in sociology. As a user, you are basically stuck with their epistemological assumptions, which are reflected in the operations and features of the program. Fortunately, the availability of a wide range of programs (e.g., NUD★IST, ETHNOGRAPH, NVivo, QUALPRO and so forth) gives the average consumer some flexibility in this regard (if you don't like the assumptions of one program, you can try another).

On the side of the positive potential for computer programs, Weitzman lists the following issues: 1. increased speed; 2. increased consistency, particularly with coding; 3. enhanced displaying features that allow researchers to visually explore their data through diagrams and color coding and so forth; and 4. the ability to consolidate all the data (notes, memos, interviews and so on) into one integrated database (p. 807). Most software programs deliver on all these promises and more.

According to Weitzman, your choice about using a software program should ultimately depend on your answers to the following questions:

1   Do you have the necessary skills and patience to work with a computer program?
2   Do you have the budget for purchasing a costly program and will you be using it more than once to justify the expense?
3   For what type of analysis will you use the program? (Adapted from Weitzman 2000: 810)

By going through this list of questions, you can decide if you should buy a program, for what purpose, and at what cost.

CHAPTER SUMMARY

This chapter began by emphasizing how the theoretical perspectives of constructionism and objectivism influence qualitative data analysis. I argued that theory is a foundational and ever-present part of the analysis. Next, I presented some of the basic steps involved in analyzing qualitative data: reducing the data, displaying the data, and drawing conclusions. The main part of the chapter then discussed the theory and practice of several major approaches to qualitative data analysis. The methods covered were content analysis, grounded theory, narrative analysis, conversation analysis, and discourse analysis.

I suggested that content analysis typically involves the analysis of textual or visual material in search of how they reflect or shape public opinion. With grounded theory the goal is to build theory from ground up, from particular observations to general concepts. I discussed Charmaz's use of grounded theory as one that is more reflexive and constructionist than the original version. Narrative was introduced as a way of sharing information with others following a particular descriptive order or genre; and its analysis was divided into narrative practice and self-presentation. In examining conversation analysis, I highlighted its connections with ethnomethodology (the study of how people create social reality and order in everyday interactions, and talk in particular), defined some of its basic concepts (membership categorization devices and turn-taking), and discussed some examples. Finally, discourse was defined as a way of knowing the social world that has practical and rhetorical implications, and its analysis was presented in terms of interactional and Foucauldian discourse analysis.

The issues of validity and reliability were reviewed in relation to the question of how we evaluate research findings. With validity, we discussed respondent validation, triangulation, and deviant case analysis. On the side of reliability, we briefly touched on intercoder reliability and test–retest reliability. Finally, I used Weitzman (2000) to summarize the advantages and disadvantages of using software programs.

My goal throughout this chapter has been to introduce basic themes and offer examples. At the end, there is no better way of learning than by doing.

SUGGESTED READINGS

Silverman's *Interpreting Qualitative Data: Methods for Analysing Talk, Text, and Interaction* (2001) and his *Doing Qualitative Research: A Practical Handbook* (2000) offer easy-to-follow, practical advice on analyzing texts and interviews. Similarly, Coffey and Atkinson's *Making Sense of Qualitative Data* (1996) is very useful for graduate students working on their theses or dissertations. If you are interested in the various theoretical positions in the field of qualitative research, I strongly recommend Gubrium and Holstein's *The New Language of Qualitative Method* (1997). Finally, for those who are contemplating the use of computer software in their analysis, both Weitzman's chapter 'Software and Qualitative Research' in the second edition of the *Handbook of Qualitative Research* (2000) as well as Seale's chapter 'Using Computers to Analyse Qualitative Data' in Silverman's *Doing Qualitative Research* (2001) offer quick and comprehensive introductions to the field.

EXERCISE 5.1

OBJECTIVE: To apply narrative analysis to understanding how personal stories are constructed.

DESCRIPTION: Write a one-page essay about how to be a good student or a 'good ____' (you can fill in the blank with a social position of your choice, like 'friend,' 'son,' or 'daughter'). Exchange your essay with a classmate who has written a similar piece. Ask her or him to analyze your work in terms of its narrative composition (see Gubrium and Holstein's research in this chapter). Do the same with your partner's paper. Compare the two analyses. Do you see any similarities or differences between the findings from the two analyses? Do they vary in terms of their footings or linkages?

EXERCISE 5.2

OBJECTIVE: To apply conversation analysis techniques to understanding how media accounts are constructed.

DESCRIPTION: Watch an interview with a politician on a TV news program (you may wish to tape the program on your VCR or record it on an audio-cassette). Pay attention to the interviewer's 'footing' or the position from which he or she asks questions (see Clayman's research discussed earlier in this chapter). Does he or she attribute controversial statements to a third party (e.g., 'It has been said by the critics that....')? Also, consider the interviewee's responses. Does the interviewee answer every question or refuse to address some? Are there many pauses in the give-and-take and do these pauses encourage the other person to elaborate on what they are saying? Who is more likely to interrupt the other speaker?

   After answering these questions, consider how the conversation could have proceeded differently. For example, what if the interviewer asked questions in the first person (e.g., 'I think you …')? Or what if the interviewee did not wait for questions and simply made statements of his or her own choosing? You could write your own script of such an interview and compare it with the original to explore the different types of social order that they reflect.

EXERCISE 5.3

OBJECTIVE: To encourage students' to evaluate the pros and cons of various methods of data analysis.

DESCRIPTION: Ask a couple if they are willing to participate in an interview about their relationship. Ask them to tell you the story of how they first met. With the couple's permission, tape-record and transcribe the interview. Analyze the results using one of the orientations discussed in this chapter. Explain your rationale for choosing a particular method and compare its relative weaknesses and strengths with the others discussed in this chapter.

6

Writing

Arguably, we are all writers. Letters or emails to friends, memos for our work colleagues, or even grocery lists are all forms of writing. The act of writing, then, is something that all literate people engage in almost daily. However, when it comes to writing research reports, we tend to become afraid and uncomfortable. We put off assignments for weeks and reluctantly turn our attention to the task of writing hours before the work is due. I hope this chapter will help reduce this fear of writing by offering concrete strategies for thinking about and producing qualitative research papers. The chapter begins with a general discussion of writing. I then review the similarities and differences between producing qualitative and quantitative research reports. Most of the chapter is devoted to the different ways in which qualitative data and findings can be represented.

The basics of writing

Writing is typically thought of as a unique, creative form of self-expression, but even in its most self-consciously creative manifestations, writing is a craft that involves endless practice and the mastery of techniques. For example, poets spend hours, if not months, writing and rewriting a short verse to perfect its meaning and impact on their readers. Creativity and technical know-how are not mutually exclusive dimensions of the craft of writing. Without technical skills the full depth of one's creative potential cannot be realized. The most frustrating writing experience is to have ideas that appear profound in one's mind but lack the necessary skills to convey them to others. To overcome this problem, we could begin by learning about the basics of writing. For the purpose of the present discussion, this means learning about the challenges that all qualitative researchers face, regardless of their topic of analysis or individual writing style. In the following pages, I address a number of common issues that you may encounter in the course of writing qualitative research projects.

Audience

Perhaps the simplest point about writing is to remember who your audience is. In its worst form, losing sight of the audience causes you to assume that your readers know the subject matter as well as you do. We cannot expect the sentences we write to make sense to the readers simply because they are meaningful to us. We do well to remember that writing is a form of communication not unlike speaking. In everyday talk, we attend to our face-to-face audience by maintaining eye contact and speaking clearly. Similarly, when you write, try to visualize your audience. Depending on who this imaginary audience is (an average reader or a learned scholar in your field), ask yourself if your sentences will make sense to them. As a general rule, you might want to try writing for the widest audience possible. If the average person could read and understand your work, it is very likely that experts in your field will also appreciate your work.

Momentum

My advisor in graduate school was fond of saying 'Writing has a momentum of its own' (personal communication with author from Gubrium, 1994). I didn't fully understand what he meant until I began writing my qualitative dissertation. As I put into writing my many ideas and organized my observation into different chapters, I quickly learned that in the process of moving from vague insights to a coherently articulated text many new leads are generated. At the same time, what I had previously thought were groundbreaking ideas turned out to be platitudes. Once I put them in writing, they were much less profound than I originally thought them to be.

For example, at the beginning of my project, I wanted to organize my dissertation around the notion that the homeless are 'postmodern heroes of our time.' The idea was inspired by interviews with homeless men who had said things like 'It sucks to be a citizen' or 'I feel sorry for the poor bastards who are enslaved by their work. I am free to sleep where I want and go where I want.' I interpreted such statements as clear rejections of the modern, capitalist premise of productive labor. Chatting in coffee shops with fellow students, I championed the cause of the homeless by quoting their anti-work statements, translating my field notes into political slogans.

Of course, eventually I had to write all of this down into a coherent document. In doing so I was presented with a serious problem. I found it impossible to transform a number of catchy statements into a full-length dissertation. Aside from a few banal declarations like 'It appears that some homeless people reject conventional notions of work,' I had nothing else to write. Given my data and level of expertise, the notion of the homeless as postmodern heroes was a dead end. On the other hand, as my writing and analysis progressed, I came across another idea that seemed more in synch with the empirical evidence. In particular, I noticed that the very concept of 'the homeless' was problematic. The men and women on the streets and in shelters viewed their circumstances from many different standpoints. Some thought of their situation as a type of personal freedom, others said they were 'miserable.' This way of analyzing and writing about my fieldwork became the foundation of my research and was further polished as the writing went on. The otherwise unmanageable mass of data started to fit into an orderly framework. In the previous chapter, it was suggested that in qualitative research data analysis and collection proceed in union. Here I would add that writing in a sense becomes a way of thinking about and analyzing the data.

Writing as an ongoing practice

The phrase 'writing as an ongoing practice' has a double meaning. On the one hand, it means that the final product of your writing efforts matures over time. Similar to the above argument about momentum, the ongoing nature of writing implies that the substance and form of a research report is not entirely predictable from the start. As you put down your thoughts on paper or type them into your computer, your writing will move in unexpected directions (though, as I caution in the next section, the challenge is to rein in your intellect; otherwise, your text could rapidly expand beyond the boundaries of the average readers' comprehension). In this sense, to say that writing is an ongoing practice is to acknowledge that this form of communication could be revised and expanded indefinitely.

Another sense of the phrase 'writing as an ongoing practice' has to do with how one could become a better writer with practice. I find it somewhat puzzling that in the social sciences the skill of writing is not taught the same way as other academic subjects are. For example, in math courses, it is understood that repeated practice is an essential part of learning the principles of this discipline. In contrast, when it comes to writing, especially in the social sciences, we assume that one either knows how to write or doesn't; writing is approached as a talent that cannot be improved. On the contrary, writing is a skill that could be bettered with practice. Don't expect your first draft to be your final one. Think of your paper as an inspiration for a sculpture that begins with a rough piece of marble and gradually becomes a recognizable figure with each strike of the chisel. To say that writing is a practice is to say that it is work. Good qualitative research papers are not written overnight no matter how insightful your research question or how interesting your data.

Knowing what not to write

Ironically, an important part of writing a qualitative research paper is knowing what not to write. A good research project will generate an enormous number of ideas. In my own research, among the many topics I became interested in were: how the homeless tell their stories, what kind of stories they tell, how the organizational context affects the storytelling, how charity work is performed in an institutional setting, the effect of inter-organizational communication on the storytelling, the survival strategies of the homeless, and friendship and family networks. Admittedly, any one of these topics could be the subject of a book. As one of my advisors reminded me, the challenge is to resist the urge to 'throw in everything but the kitchen sink,' as the saying goes. Not every good idea has to be used in the same paper. Decide what you need to make one project work and save the rest for another paper.

Proofreading

When it comes to improving your writing, nothing works better for catching typos and refining your arguments than proofreading. Without it, relatively minor problems, like a missing or a misspelled word here and there, could frustrate your reader and cause them to assume a much less favorable attitude toward your work. Don't be shy about asking others to read your work and comment on it. You should especially solicit the input of readers who have expertise in the area about which you are writing. If you don't have this luxury, try reading your paper aloud. If you have a hard time verbalizing what you wrote, the chances are people will have difficulty reading it.

In recent years, we have become more dependent on computer word-processors (e.g., WordPerfect or MS Word) for catching our writing errors. While extremely useful and convenient, these programs are not foolproof. The spell-check feature can be particularly unreliable and lead to very embarrassing mistakes. For example, several years ago, I submitted a paper for publication to a journal. In the abstract of this paper, I inserted the following sentence, 'The data for this paper was gathered at a pubic conference.' You may have noticed that the word 'pubic,' although correctly spelled, does not fit the sentence. What I meant to say was 'a public conference.' (I am sure the journal reviewers had a good laugh at my expense.) Don't rely on computer software to catch all your errors. Unfortunately, the technology is not that fully developed yet. A correctly spelled word could be semantically incorrect, and the existing computer programs have no way of detecting errors that involve the meaning of a word in a given sentence.

As a whole, attention to these general features of writing could improve any paper. In the next section, I discuss some of the basic differences and similarities between writing quantitative and qualitative papers.

Writing a research paper

In its most basic form a sociology research paper answers a question posed about society using empirical data. For example, you could write a paper about *why* some teenagers abuse drugs, or *why* some young college students cheat on their exams. You can also ask *how* questions like: How is mental illness represented in Hollywood films? Some research papers are based on *what* questions, such as: What is the rate of unemployment in a given country? In practice, however, there is a good deal of overlap between why, how, and what questions. Your inquiry about the rate of employment, for example, leads to *why* it might be low or high. Similarly, looking into why teenagers do drugs may not be possible without understanding *what* drugs they abuse and *how*.

Regardless of the type of question that is posed in a research paper, the answer is going to involve empirical evidence. For example, in showing how mental illness is represented in cinema, we need to cite specific movies that portray this topic in one form or another. Similarly, when writing about teen drug abuse, we have to demonstrate cases of abuse and provide theoretical interpretations for them. As discussed in Chapter 1, the empirical data for sociological research could be placed into two broad categories: qualitative and quantitative. The significance of this distinction for writing research papers is that procedures for presenting your findings and arguments could vary depending on the type of data you are working with. Let us briefly consider some of these differences.

The quantitative approach

The numerical nature of the quantitative research paves the way for a standardized approach to data analysis and writing. Typically, the analysis is based on statistical techniques and the data are listed in tables. The accompanying written text summarizes and highlights the content of the tables. Table 6.1 is an example of a numerical table and the writing format that accompanies it.

TABLE 6.1   *Frequency distribution of race*

Racial category	Frequency	Percentage
Black	120	15
White	700	78
Other	115	7
Totals	1000	100

Source: A sub-sample from the General Social Survey 1998

The accompanying text would read:

> Table 6.1 shows the frequency distribution of the respondents' race. The majority of respondents (78%) are white with blacks forming the next largest category (15%) followed by other racial groups (7%).

As seen in this example, the words in a quantitative paper describe the numbers. In a more sophisticated research paper, where several variables are compared, the written text relates the numbers to the arguments stated in the introduction of the paper. These arguments, or educated guesses, about potential relationships between variables are referred to as *hypotheses*. In short, in quantitative research, the writing is organized as follows:

1   introduction of the problem and research hypotheses;
2   description of the methods by which the data was collected and the variables measured;
3   presentation of the numerical findings in the form of tables; and
4   concluding remarks that both summarize and point to future possibilities for research on the same or a related topic.

The qualitative approach

Qualitative and quantitative papers are similar in that they both try to answer research questions using empirical data. The difference is that instead of numerical information, qualitative research is mostly based on descriptive data. This means rather than words elaborating on the meaning of numbers, in qualitative research we have used words to explain other words. It should be noted that for some qualitative researchers, such as content analysts (see Chapter 5), respondents' descriptions are transformed into numbers; therefore, their written reports follow the same format as quantitative studies (words elaborate on the significance of numerical information). However, for most other qualitative researchers, the quality of social life is linked with descriptions offered by the researcher. Consider, for example, the following analysis and related data, which are from a qualitative study of court proceedings to determine who is in need of involuntary commitment to a mental institution.

> Descriptions like one's gender can be made consequential, as in the case of Kathleen Wells, who became a candidate for commitment when she was found living in a large cardboard carton beneath a railroad overpass. . . . In presenting her arguments for commitment, the County Attorney . . . invoked the candidate patient's gender as a framework for seeing this arrangement as especially untenable [the data follows]:

> Now I know Miss Wells claims that this [the cardboard box] is as good as the subsidized public housing programs... , but we have to consider more than its construction aspects....You can't allow a woman to be exposed to all the other things that go on out there under the [railroad] tracks. Many of those men have lived like that for years, but we're talking about a woman here. A sick and troubled woman who doesn't realize the trouble she's asking for. She simply cannot live like that...

In this case, the County Attorney explicitly argued that the proposed living arrangement, while perhaps being tolerable for men, was inappropriate for a woman. (Adapted from Holstein 1992: 30)

As shown in this example, in qualitative texts, the analysis typically begins with a background description that sets the stage for the introduction of the data. After presenting the data, more analysis and explanatory remarks follow. This is not fundamentally different from the way quantitative analysis is written. Again, the key difference is that in most qualitative texts words are used to explain other words, whereas in quantitative research this relationship is between words and numbers.

In the next section, we explore a number of formats for organizing a qualitative research paper from start to finish.

Styles of presenting qualitative research papers

There are many styles for writing a qualitative research paper. Some researchers opt for thematically organized style, with each section representing a different concept. Others, especially ethnographers, write their reports as stories with a set of characters, a plot, and a setting. For the novice writer this kind of freedom and flexibility can be overwhelming. The obvious question for many beginners is: Where do I begin and end a qualitative paper?

The best way to reduce your anxiety about writing is to begin with a good research question. As the saying about computers goes: 'garbage in, garbage out.' It is hard to transform a loosely stated or illogical research question into a good paper. How does one judge a 'good research question?' Begin by making sure that you can actually collect data about your research topic. If you already have the data, ask a question that is relevant to the information at hand. Recently, a student in my research methods class asked if he could conduct a qualitative research project on the effect of race on criminal behavior. He indicated that he found the in-depth interview approach 'interesting' and thought that race and crime would be 'exciting' topics for a research project. I agreed that the topic was indeed very important, but I had to remind the student of a number of potential problems. First, I asked him to explain why he thought his study should be done qualitatively. There are many large numerical data sets and statistical techniques that could be used to answer a question of this kind, so why do it qualitatively? I also asked him if he had given any thought to where and how he would recruit respondents for his project, and if he saw any ethical problems with asking people about their possible involvement in crime.

Finally, I wanted to know if he had enough time to collect and analyze the data and write up the findings all in the course of one semester (roughly four months). After our discussion, the student decided to take on a more manageable project.

The point of this story is that important topics don't necessarily make for good research questions. You should also consider other factors such as:

- the suitability of the method
- the length of time available for the project
- the expected length and purpose of the paper
- ethical problems

It is likely that the focus of your study might be refined as the project goes on, but if you are not at all clear on how your data will inform potential readers about a given issue, then writing a coherent paper will be next to impossible.

With a sound research question in mind and after collecting and analyzing your data, you are ready to report your findings. The following discussion provides three possible ways for writing a typical research paper.

Standard model

The most widely used mode of writing a qualitative research paper organizes the text into four elements: *introduction, methods, analysis* and *conclusion*. Think of each section as answering a different set of questions about your project. Accordingly, the introduction addresses the following:

1   What is the topic of your paper?
2   Have there been previous studies on this topic? If so, offer a short summary of the most recent ones in terms of their research questions, data, and findings.

The goal of the introduction section is to let your readers know what you are researching and what other researchers have said about your topic.

The second part of a standard research paper discusses the methods. This part tells the readers how you did your study. Specifically, it provides detailed answers to these questions:

1   What was the size of the sample for the study?
2   How did you collect this sample?
3   Where did you collect this sample?
4   How did you analyze your data?

The specific content of this section varies depending on the data collection technique and type of analysis. For example, in writing their methods section, ethnographers describe the setting or the research site in great length. They want their readers to know how they gained entry to the site, how they established relationships with their respondents, and what questions they asked from them and under what circumstances. On the other hand, a researcher who does survey-style, closed-ended interviews is unlikely to put as much emphasis on the setting. For this kind of researcher, the discussion of methods will be mostly about what questions were asked from how many people. A general guide for writing the methods section is to provide enough detail for other researchers to replicate your study if they so choose.

The analysis follows next. Also referred to as the results or the findings, this section presents your data and its interpretation with the goal of providing answers to these questions:

1   What is the empirical evidence for this study?
2   What social processes are revealed by the data?
3   How does it support the researcher's claims about a particular sociological topic or process?

As discussed in Chapter 5, in qualitative research, there are many ways of analyzing data. Irrespective of the type of analysis you conduct, in reporting your findings you should draw clear, logical connections between the empirical data and your interpretations. Do not assume that your readers share your point of view. Take them by the hand, so to speak, and walk them through the data. Refer to the data as much as possible to support your arguments without overwhelming your readers with large, under-analyzed excerpts.

The last part of a typical research paper is the conclusion or the discussion. This section should include the following:

1   A brief summary of your project (the research question, methods, and findings)
2   The social or political implications of your findings (i.e., how will your study be of interest to ordinary people or policymakers?)
3   Ways in which you would improve your study if you had more time and money.

To put it simply, the conclusion states: 'This is what I said I was going to do, this is how I did it, and these were the findings. If I had the time and the resources to do it over, these are the changes I would make to my research design.'

Most other styles of writing research papers are variations of this standard theme. What changes is the style of writing and the degree of emphasis placed on each of the four components (i.e., introduction, methods, analysis, and conclusion). Next we look at how a paper could be organized around concepts or themes.

Thematically organized model

Another way of writing a qualitative paper is to use themes or concepts from your research as headings for the paper. A good example of this style of presentation is found in Loseke and Fawcett's article 'Appealing Appeals: Constructing Moral Worthiness, 1912-1927.' In their analysis of *New York*

Times stories about candidate charity recipients, the authors organize their work along the following headings:

> Appealing Appeals: Constructing Moral Worthiness, 1912–1917
> [This is the title of the paper and is followed by an introductory discussion.]
> READING THE CAMPAIGNS
> [The methods section is inserted here.]
> THE TRUTH OF THE NEEDIEST
> [This is where the analysis of data begins in relation to the concepts of 'need' and 'morality']
> Producing Need
> Producing Morality
> [Subheadings are used to further elaborate on the concept.]
>   *Morality of Biography*
>   *Morality of Activity*
>   *Morality of Motivation*
> MORALITY AND THE INSTITUTIONAL ORDER
> [More data analysis about the institutional context of constructing morality]
> MORALITY PRODUCTION AND THE APPARATUS OF RULING
> [This is where the authors summarize and conclude their findings]
> (Adapted from Loseke and Fawcett 1995: 61–67)

Writing your paper this way does not mean you can skip the core elements of a standard research paper (i.e., introduction, methods, analysis, and conclusion). As my bracketed comments suggest, a thematically organized paper still contains these essential components under differently named headings. The main advantage of this style of presentation is that it enables you to give priority to your chosen concepts. The headings provide substantive information about the research, signaling to the reader what topical issue will be discussed next. The challenge of this approach is that it requires some creativity and a good command of your data and analysis. Comparatively, it is easier to simply use generic headings like 'Introduction' or 'Methods.' In practice, most qualitative papers in sociology, especially those published in research journals, use hybrids of the standard and the thematic models. So you might see a heading like 'Analysis' followed by more conceptually driven subheadings. Let us now consider a less traditional model of writing.

Story-driven models

Some qualitative sociologists see writing as a type of storytelling, and in presenting their research, they emphasize descriptions of characters, the different 'scenes' in which the data was collected, the author's reflections and the roles she or he enacted in the story. In some forms of this method of writing, the authors themselves become the center of the research narrative. For example, Ellis and Bochner narrate their personal experience with abortion in this way:

> Telling and Performing Personal Stories: The Constraints of Choice in Abortion
> [Title followed by an introduction to the research topic and procedures]
> The Story
> Scene 1: The Pregnancy Test and the Test of Pregnancy
> Scene 2: Making the Decision
> Scene 3: Dealing with the Decision
> Scene 4: The Preabortion Procedure
> Scene 5: The Abortion
> Epilogue
>
> (Adapted from Ellis and Bochner 1992: 70–101)

As seen in this example, this model does not adhere to the writing conventions of a standard research paper. This has led to some controversy about whether this way of representing social experience passes the litmus test of scientific writing, and more important, if it should be considered sociology at all (see Flaherty et al. 2002, Gubrium and Holstein 1997b, and Marvasti and Faircloth 2002 for a review of the debates surrounding the question of representation in qualitative research).

Nonetheless, the idea of storytelling through sociological research is not entirely new. In fact, most ethnographies are narratives of sort about a person entering a site and reporting their experiences, as in the case of Whyte's classic ethnography *Street Corner Society* (1949). To some degree, the decision to write your paper in a narrative style should depend on how you collected your data and what kind of data you collected. For example, ethnographic methods are better suited for storied research reports (for a discussion of ethnographic techniques see Chapter 3). The research procedures readily lend themselves to the mainstays of storytelling (e.g., characters and settings). The story could begin with the researcher entering the field and end with her or his departure. By contrast, it is more difficult to write a survey research project as a story.

Three points about writing research papers

There are three things you should keep in mind when writing a qualitative research paper. First, ask a workable research question. In theory, just about anything could be studied qualitatively, but in practice, some topics are better suited for this method of research than others. If you are interested in the rate of alcoholism among college students on your campus, a survey-based quantitative project might be the answer. On the other hand, if you want to know about the social processes through which students come to see themselves as 'alcoholics,' in-depth interviews or an ethnography of life on a college campus might produce more fruitful results.

Second, do not approach writing and data collection as separate parts of your research paper. Write everything down as you collect your data. This means everything from conversations with teachers and friends, to your personal feelings about the project, to circumstances under which the data was collected. Much of this material may not be included in the final draft of your paper, but at the very least, the continuous recording of all this information will hone your writing skills. If you don't begin writing until the data collection is complete, your original research question might seem like a needle in a haystack of data. Continuous writing helps you stay on track and focused. Also if you like to talk about your work with friends, make the conversations more productive by tape-recording them, or take notes as you are talking. This might seem pretentious but unless recorded, the useful ideas that are generated in the flow of a stimulating conversation could be lost forever.

Third, learn how to balance your time between writing and data collection: For many students, collecting and talking about their data is more enjoyable than writing. It is more fun to chat with fellow students about your ideas and tell anecdotes from your field experiences than it is to put these thoughts into writing. Force yourself to write as the project moves on. When you have many pages of notes and data, it may be time to devote more effort to piecing together the first draft of the paper.

CHAPTER SUMMARY

This chapter began by exploring general aspects of writing (e.g., momentum, writing as an ongoing practice, and the importance of proofreading). Next, some basic distinctions between writing quantitative and qualitative research papers were discussed. I suggested that the two share an emphasis on reporting findings from empirical research. The main difference between them is that with quantitative research the written text references numerical information, whereas in qualitative research words are often used to elaborate on the sociological significance of other words. Also, quantitative research papers tend to be more standardized or formulaic in their presentations than their qualitative counterparts. Three styles of writing qualitative research papers were discussed: the traditional, the conceptually organized, and the story-driven models. The traditional model contains the following components: introduction, methods, analysis, and conclusion. The conceptual model gives priority to themes and concepts in the organization of the paper. Finally, the story-driven model is written in a narrative form, with special attention to the story's characters and settings. The chapter ended with the following recommendations:

1   consider the suitability of your research question for a qualitative project;
2   write as you collect data; and
3   balance your time between writing and data collection.

SUGGESTED READINGS

For those interested in the more theoretical dimensions of writing, Richardson's book *Writing Strategies: Researching Diverse Audiences* (1990b) offers an assessment of qualitative research as a mode of representing reality. Alternatively, Wolcott's *Writing Up Qualitative Research* (2001) and Silverman's chapters on writing and publishing in *Doing Qualitative Research* (2000) offer reader-friendly and comprehensive advice.

EXERCISE 6.1

OBJECTIVE: To develop a research proposal based on the steps outlined in this chapter.

DESCRIPTION: Write a two-page proposal for a qualitative research paper consisting of the following four sections, each about a page long.

Part one: Describe your topic and research question. Be specific about what dimensions of a particular topic you are interested in investigating. For example, if you are interested in researching crime, explain what kind of crime (e.g., drug abuse, violent crime, or property crime). Be equally clear about your question. In the example of crime, the question could be something like: How do shoplifters justify their actions?

Part two: Explain what research techniques will be used for this study. If you are planning to do interviews, discuss where and how you will recruit subjects and how many will be included in the study. Also include samples of the questions you plan to ask your respondents. Similarly, if you are considering an ethnographic project, describe your research site, how you will gain entry, how long your project will last, and other relevant information. Be sure to include a discussion on why your topic could best be studied using the method you have chosen and what type of analysis will be applied to the data (you may choose one of the approaches discussed in Chapter 5).

Part three: Briefly discuss the expected results of your project. What do you think your project will reveal about your topic of interest?

Part four: Discuss the practical implications or usefulness of your project. For example, if your study is about shoplifting, how can it be used by police officers or storeowners to deal with this problem?

EXERCISE 6.2

OBJECTIVE: To enhance students' writing skills through regular practice.

DESCRIPTION: Practice your writing skills by starting a diary called *Stories of The Day*. Everyday record an interesting event that happened to you or someone you know. Write these stories as if you were verbally sharing them with an audience. Make your descriptions detailed and clear. Don't assume your audience is familiar with the characters and the settings.

EXERCISE 6.3

OBJECTIVES: To encourage students to solicit feedback from their peers and to evaluate their writing based on how well it is understood by others.

DESCRIPTION: Ask someone to read aloud a short paper you wrote for a class. Pay attention to how they might struggle with your sentences or writing style. Take notes on things you can correct to make your paper sound better. Make these corrections and ask your friend to reread the paper. How has your paper improved?

7

Ethics in Qualitative Research

In investigating people's experiences, the researcher enters a relationship with those she or he studies. The ethics of social research have to do with the nature of the researcher's responsibilities in this relationship, or the things that should or should not be done regarding the people being observed and written about. This is not significantly different from what we do in other relationships. We try to be polite, treat people with respect, and don't do or say anything that will harm them. Good manners are a good beginning, but actual research scenarios may require guidelines that go beyond common courtesy. My own fieldwork at a homeless shelter presented a number of ethical dilemmas.

For example, there was Gregory (pseudonyms are used here to protect the identities of respondents). He was a middle-aged white man who lived on the streets near the shelter. Gregory was a talented poet and author who suffered from alcoholism. As we became more familiar with each other, he began asking me to buy him beer. So as a matter of courtesy, from time to time I paid for his bar tab. Unfortunately, Gregory's drinking became worse and his requests for money to support his habit became more frequent and direct. He started leaving messages on my home answering machine begging me to meet him at a bar to pay his tab. I finally decided that it was unethical for me to support his addiction and stopped helping him. The next phone call I received from Gregory was from a local jail where he was being held for shoplifting a bottle of beer from a convenience store. He wanted me to make arrangements for his legal defense. I went to visit Gregory at the jail and told him there was very little I could do for him. Several weeks later he was released and subsequently left for New York City. I did not hear from him again.

During my research, I also met a homeless man named Tony. He was in his mid-twenties and had a passion for movie making. Since part of my project involved videotaping interviews with the street people around the shelter, I asked Tony if he would operate the camcorder while I asked questions from the respondents. He accepted my request and took the work very seriously. On one occasion, I asked Tony to help me edit some of our raw footage into a short documentary. We showed the work to a group of college students at a gathering in support of the homeless. It was well received and Tony was delighted to be part of the project.

Tony also acted as my informant, taking me to places where the homeless spent their time. To return the favor, I helped Tony fill out his applications for a local college and gave him advice on applying for government-subsidized financial aid. As I saw it, this was a fair arrangement where we both benefited, but I gradually realized that Tony believed his participation in my research would help him become an independent filmmaker. At one point, he suggested that we edit the tapes into a short independent film about the homeless. I did not object to his ambitions but thought that his expectations about our collaborations were unrealistic. So I gently reminded him that I was mainly collecting data for a dissertation. If he were hurt by this, he hid it well. His interest in my work dissipated over time. Tony eventually secured a job at a local movie theater as an usher. On the occasional Saturday night when I went to see a movie where he worked, Tony would get my attention from a distance by shouting, 'Hey, when are we going to work on that film together?' I would smile and say with embarrassment, 'I don't know.'

Thinking about these stories may cause you to wonder if you would have handled these situations differently. Is it possible that I was not forthcoming enough about the purpose of my research with Tony? Perhaps I was too involved with Gregory and should have severed my ties with him much earlier. The point of these stories for the present discussion is that qualitative research involves working with people and making ethical choices about how to treat them. In this chapter, we will discuss some of the central issues related to ethics in qualitative research. I begin by learning about the basic principles that concern all researchers when working with human participants. I then discuss how informed consent documents are developed and administered in order to protect research participants and end this chapter by considering the limitations of the informed consent protocol as employed in qualitative research.

The basic principles

Today most researchers, regardless of their discipline or methodological orientation, recognize that when working with human subjects (as opposed to cultural artifacts or objects), certain steps must be taken to protect the dignity and safety of the research participants. However, the wide acceptance and implementation of this ethical awareness is a relatively new development. As recently as the 1970s, highly unethical social and medical studies were being conducted in the United States. In one of the most troubling examples of unscrupulous research, a group of 399 African-American men afflicted with syphilis unknowingly became participants in a medical experiment (Jones 1981: 1–23). From the 1930s to 1970s, the physicians assigned to these men deliberately did not treat them for their ailment, even after penicillin was developed and could have been used as a cure. Instead, the patients were secretly experimented on to examine the effects of untreated syphilis. By the time this U.S. Public Health Service study was exposed and subsequently terminated, many of the patients whose condition had gone untreated for years had either died horribly or become more severely ill.

Instances of unethical research are not limited to medical experiments. Among social scientists in the United States, a well-known example of unethical research is Humphreys' *Tearoom Trade* (1970). Humphreys studied anonymous homosexual encounters in semi-public places. Specifically, he was interested in the background of men who had sex with other men in public restrooms. After positioning himself in a restroom in a city park, he gained the trust of the men who frequented it by acting as a lookout for them while they engaged in sexual activities. Humphreys secretly recorded their license plate numbers, and with the help of the police discovered who they were and where they lived. Months later, he visited the men in their homes disguised as a medical survey researcher. He gathered additional information about these men and their families and subsequently published his research in a book that was widely praised before questions were raised about its ethics. One of the main findings of his work was that many of the men in his study were married and of middle class background – a discovery that was made possible through the covert invasion of the subjects' privacy.

Such flagrant abuses of research subjects in the name of science have led to the establishment of specific codes of conduct. While these may vary across disciplines and national boundaries, there are a number of general principles that most researchers would agree with. The following presents a brief review of these principles (i.e., voluntary participation, protection of research participants, potential benefit to participants and guidelines on the use of deception).

Voluntary participation

Participation in a research project should be voluntary; you should not psychologically or physically force your subjects to take part in your research. Let us consider a number of scenarios that run the risk of violating this principle. Suppose a sociologist, Professor Johnson, asks his students to fill out a short-answer questionnaire for a course on social stratification and poverty. The required assignment involves writing about your personal or family experiences with poverty. You are supposed to answer questions like: 'Have you and your family ever experienced economic hardship? If so, describe how you felt about it?;' 'In your view, what has been the psychological impact of such an experience on you?;' and 'If you have not personally experienced financial difficulties, you may answer these questions about a relative or an acquaintance.' Professor Johnson informs that excerpts from the survey questionnaires will be used anonymously for a research project about college students' attitudes toward poverty. Has the principle of voluntary participation been violated in this case?

Some would say the answer is yes. Given that the assignment is required, the students' decision not to participate most certainly will hurt their grades. They *have to* participate regardless of how they feel about their personal accounts being used for research purposes. On the other hand, if Professor Johnson offered several assignment choices, only one of which was the autobiographical one, then the decision to partake in the project is voluntary. Alternatively, Johnson might make the research voluntary by announcing that the answers may not be used without your consent.

Similarly, the principle of voluntary participation can be violated when you lure the indigent into a study by offering them monetary rewards. For example, to get an interview with a homeless person, a researcher might offer them five dollars. Is this ethical? Many would argue that it isn't because asking the poor to participate in a study in exchange for money is the moral equivalent of asking a starving person to answer a few questions in exchange for a plate of food. What is the solution? One possibility is to solicit interviews without any rewards. Another approach is to contact their service providers and ask if they know of anyone who is willing to be interviewed.

How about when you are observing people in public places such as malls or restaurants? Do you need to approach each patron for permission to observe them? The general consensus is that what people do in public places is by definition there for all to observe. The same guideline applies to public statements. If in a published newspaper editorial I refer to my personal experiences, you don't need my permission to use words that are already public domain (obviously, you have to cite the author and the source). What if the interviewee is a child or someone who is mentally incapacitated? In these cases, the recommendation is to gain consent from a parent or a guardian before proceeding with the research.

As these examples indicate, it is sometimes difficult to assess the degree to which the subjects' participation is completely voluntary. While a strictly legalistic interpretation of the phrase 'voluntary participation' might be useful in some cases, you may ultimately have to rely on your own judgment and sense of morality to determine if the person you are researching is fully aware of the implications of their involvement in your study.

Protection of the research participants

Even if your respondents voluntarily take part in your study, they may not be in a position to fully appreciate the potential harm they could suffer from their participation. For example, after obtaining permission from members of a support group for the chronically depressed, a researcher proceeds to conduct interviews about the sources of their mental illness. One of the questions that comes up during the interview is whether or not the respondent has been a victim of child abuse. Specifically, the researcher asks, 'Have you been sexually or physically abused by a relative or an acquaintance? If so, please describe how this happened and when?' Suppose the respondent tries to answer this question and in the process has to recall a very painful past. After the interview, the respondent becomes even more depressed and tries to commit suicide. Is the researcher to blame for this unfortunate event, given that the participation was completely voluntary?

In this example, it is likely that the respondent did not know the consequences of participating in the study. Given the sensitive nature of child abuse, perhaps our researcher should have taken precautionary steps to terminate the interview if the respondent appeared overly emotional. At the very least, the research participants should have been informed in advance about the types of questions they would be asked and reminded that they have the option not to answer certain questions or to end the interview whenever they wish. In theory, researchers should take every reasonable measure to protect their subjects from harm, but in reality, it is impossible to anticipate every risk. One reason for this is that your study might affect respondents in different ways. In the example above, for some participants talking about their past might indeed be therapeutic, whereas for others it might be traumatic. In the end, it is your responsibility as a researcher to minimize potential harm as much as possible. This means that in some cases you may have to abandon your research idea altogether because the risk of harm is too great. For example, psychologists may find it very interesting to study the effect of social isolation on children as this would teach us a great deal about the importance of socialization. However, the thought of separating innocent children from all their loved ones is unconscionable no matter what the scientific merit of the study.

Confidentiality and anonymity

An important part of protecting your research subjects is guarding their privacy; revealing the identities of your respondents could harm them. For example, if you were researching homosexual couples who preferred to keep their lifestyle secret from their relatives, disclosing their names would seriously damage their family relationships. Or suppose you were interviewing high school students about drug use and they reported that they experimented with marijuana. If your respondents were exposed, they could be expelled from school and possibly face legal charges. Privacy is also a concern when dealing with more conventional topics. For example, in an ethnography of a hospital, the nurses might disclose their opinions about the physicians they work with. A nurse might gripe about how a certain doctor is always late for her/his appointments. Revealing the respondent's identity in this case may result in her/his dismissal from work.

Confidentiality and anonymity are two aspects of the privacy issue. Confidentiality means that the identity of the respondent will not be disclosed to anyone. So when you refer to a particular research participant in your writing, as I did earlier in this chapter when discussing Gregory and Tony, you keep their identities hidden by using fictional names. You should also try to disguise other identifying information, such as where they live or work. For example, if you are doing your research in Gainesville, Florida, you might refer to the location as 'a small city in the southeastern United States.' Or if your data was collected at a hospital named Bethesda Memorial, you should change the name to something like 'Clairmount Memorial.' Overall, confidentiality implies that, except for the researcher, no one else will know the identity of the participants.

Anonymity means that even the researcher does not know the identity of the respondents. In qualitative studies where you observe people in various settings and interview them face-to-face, complete anonymity is impossible – in most cases you meet research participants in person. Nevertheless, certain steps can be taken toward providing subjects with limited anonymity. For example, if the interviews are taped, do not label the cassettes with the respondents' actual names. Either use fictional names or organize your tapes using randomly assigned numbers. Similarly, you can create a set of pseudonyms for all your research participants and use them in your notes instead of their real names. It is likely that over time you forget what their real names were and remember them only by the fictional names you assign to them.

Benefit to the research participants

We rely on research respondents to provide the raw material for our analysis and reports. They share with us their time and social experiences, but usually they are not financially compensated for their contributions. So, how do we pay them back? The ethical concern here is to ensure that the research-subject relationship is mutually beneficial. We don't want to exploit subjects or respondents, taking from them without giving anything back. To make this arrangement more equitable, the research project could be designed in a way that benefits the subjects and their communities.

For example, let's say you plan to study how children construct ethnic or racial identities for themselves and others by positioning yourself at a daycare center as a volunteer and observing how children interact with one another on the playground, which is precisely what Van Ausdale and Feagin did in their book *The First R: How Children Learn Race and Racism* (2002). Their study provides disturbing, but eye-opening, accounts of how young children use racist epithets in reference to their peers. How was this project beneficial to the research participants? Van Ausdale and Feagin reason that in the end their work indirectly benefits the children by informing parents and educators about potential problems with the way their charges learn about and practice race and ethnicity.

Sociological studies that more explicitly encourage respondents' full participation in all phases of the research process with the goal of bettering their lives are referred to as 'participatory research.' As Small notes:

> Participatory researchers are openly and explicitly political. Their ideology emphasizes large-scale structural forces, conflicts of interest, and the need to overcome oppression and inequality through transforming the existing social order. The lack of access to useful and valued forms of knowledge by oppressed or disenfranchised people is viewed as a major problem that can be overcome through the research process. (1995: 944)

As a whole, qualitative studies can be beneficial in three important ways (Silverman 2001: 271–81). First, they could help increase awareness, and stimulate debate, about public policies. Research on the health care system, for example, has provided much useful information about needed improvements. Second, qualitative research could make people more aware of their choices. In the example above, Van Ausdale and Feagin's research encourages another choice for constructing children's racial identities, one that is more inclusive and tolerant. Finally, qualitative research provides 'new perspectives' on old problems. For example, my research questions the conventional profile of 'the homeless' as being helpless victims of poverty, mental illness, and drug abuse. I suggest that contrary to these stereotypical representations, some homeless people make rational choices about their lives, particularly in regard to where and how they receive social services (Marvasti 2003).

The ethical principles of voluntary participation and protecting and benefiting the participants are sometimes addressed through a formal protocol, which is briefly reviewed in the next section.

The informed consent model

To address these basic ethical issues in working with human subjects, sometimes researchers use what is referred to as an *informed consent*. This includes written or verbal statements that provide research participants with a general description of the research project along with its potential harms and benefits. Some academic institutions in the United States ask all researchers to make use of the informed consent protocol under the guidelines of the office of Institutional Review Boards (IRB). An IRB is a committee composed of representatives from various departments in a university and is charged with reviewing all research projects involving human subjects. Before allowing a study to proceed, IRB might request further clarification or changes to the design and implementation of the research. Let us consider the elements of a written informed consent.

Developing a written consent form

A written consent form should address all the ethical concerns introduced earlier in this chapter. Namely, it should emphasize that:

- Participation is voluntary.
- No harm will come to the participants (if there is any risk of harm, it should be clearly described).
- The participants' privacy will be protected (steps that will be taken to ensure protection of privacy should be listed specifically).

Think of the informed consent as a contract that specifies your ethical responsibilities to the respondents. If your research is conducted under the auspices of an academic institution in the United States and the IRB has approved your project, violations of the informed consent agreement may have legal ramifications for you and your school.

Below is an example of an informed consent form from a study that my colleague and I developed for our research on Middle Eastern Americans.

INFORMED CONSENT FORM

Title of Project: Middle Eastern Lives in the United States

1   *Purpose of the study*: The purpose of this study is to bring to light the existence of Middle Easterners in America and to show the human complexity of their lives. The work gives special attention to how members of this ethnic group cope with, resist and combat discrimination.

2   *Procedures to be followed*: We request that you answer a number of in-depth questions in this audiotaped focus group or interview. Afterwards, you will be asked to complete a short survey questionnaire. We expect your entire participation will take approximately 90 minutes.

3   *Discomforts and risks*: As with any research study, the only possible discomfort you might experience from participation in this study is that you could be uncomfortable answering certain questions. For this reason, you may decline to answer any or all of our questions, or you may stop participating at any time.

4   *Benefits*: This is an opportunity for Middle Easterners like yourself to present a balanced and unbiased perspective on their lives.

5   *Statement of confidentiality*: Your participation in this research is confidential. Only the researchers will have access to the audiotape and transcription of your interview along with any other information that discloses your identity in this research project. All these materials will be stored at Dr. Marvasti's residence and will be destroyed by the end of the year 2003. No identifying labels will be attached to the audiotape (the audiotape will not be associated with your identity). Also, in the event of publication of this research, no personally identifying information will be disclosed. Your name will be changed to an alias in any publications or reports, and any details which might identify you will also be removed.

6   *Right to ask questions*: You can ask questions about the research. The people in charge will answer your questions. Contact Dr. Marvasti or Dr. McKinney.

7   *Voluntary participation*: Your participation is completely voluntary. You may refuse to answer any questions you do not wish to answer. You may end your participation at any time without penalty by telling the researchers.

You must be 18 years of age or older to consent to participation in this research study. If you consent to participate in this research study and to the terms above, please sign your name and indicate the date below. You will be given a copy of this consent form to keep for your records. (Adapted from Marvasti and McKinney, forthcoming)

Before each interview, we present our respondents with a more expanded version of this form. Without the respondents' signature and approval, we do not proceed. The people contacted for our study have expressed that they are comfortable with the safeguards that are put in place for their protection. However, such contractual agreements are not without problems. The next discussion considers some of these shortcomings.

The limitations of the informed consent model as applied to qualitative research

The informed consent approach is very useful in specifying ethical boundaries for researchers. However, these guidelines are based on the assumptions of quantitative, survey research, where questions are asked from a known sample with very little variation from one respondent to another. The problem is that in qualitative research sometimes the interview questions and the focus of the project itself changes in the course of the study. Depending on the circumstances, one interview may be very different from another. This is especially true for in-depth interviews in which follow-up questions emerge spontaneously in reaction to respondent's comments. Since one cannot anticipate the exact direction the interview will take, it is impossible to inform fully the respondent about the focus of the study in advance. Similar problems arise in ethnographic studies (see Chapter 3), where in the course of your observations, you come in contact with many people in many settings. In general, in the context of qualitative research, two factors impede the full implementation of informed consent guidelines:

1. it may be difficult to define precisely the characteristics and number of research participants in advance, and
2. the focus of the study and the related research questions may undergo changes over the course of the project.

These challenges have led some qualitative researchers to raise fundamental questions about the feasibility of informed consent. For example, Lawton (2002), in her study of dying patients at a hospice (a medical/residential facility designed for the care of the terminally ill), underscores the many ethical concerns that informed consent guidelines fail to address. Specifically, she asks how informed is informed consent? Lawton makes the case that many of the dying patients she studied were not alert enough to fully understand the purpose of her research. At the same time, she notes that it may be necessary to continually remind research participants of the informed consent agreement since in prolonged studies, such as ethnographies, the participants may be observed many times in many situations for different purposes.

Overall, while the principles of informing and protecting respondents play a significant role in quantitative and qualitative research, there may be differences in the way these guidelines are implemented for the two approaches. Quantitative research is more inductive, it starts with a set of clearly stated

TABLE 7.1   *Silverman's three research roles*

Role	Politics	Commitment
Scholar	Liberal	Knowledge for knowledge's sake, protected by scholar's conscience
State counselor	Bureaucratic	Social engineering or enlightenment for policymakers
Partisan	Leftwing Rightwing	Knowledge to support both a political theory and political practice

Source: adapted from Silverman 2001: 261

questions and hypotheses and proceeds to data collection and analysis. Consequently, quantitative or survey researchers are in a position to inform their respondents from the start about exactly what they plan to study and how. By contrast, qualitative research tends to be more deductive, proceeding from observations to general statements. For qualitative researchers, it is more difficult to completely inform participants about the purpose and the specific direction of the inquiries at the onset of the research project.

Research roles and audiences

Should researchers allow personal or political values to enter their work? In this regard, according to Silverman (2001: 259–66), sociologists can assume three different roles. First, there is the position of the 'scholar.' In this capacity, the researcher is interested in science for the sake of science and judges the study's relevance and ethics based on his or her own moral principles. As Silverman suggests, this position is best represented by Max Weber, who 'insisted on the primacy of the individual's conscience as a basis for action' (2001: 261). The second research role is that of a 'state counselor.' Here, the goal is to work closely with interested policymakers. In this role, sociologists might be viewed as social engineers who assist state bureaucrats in a joint effort to create a 'better' society. Finally, there is the 'partisan' role, where the sociologist sides with a particular group. In Silverman's words, 'the partisan seeks to provide the theoretical and factual resources for a political struggle aimed at transforming the assumptions through which both political and administrative games are played' (2001: 265). The partisan role is best captured in an often quoted statement by Becker in which he asks sociologists, 'Whose side are we on?' (Becker 1967: 239). For Becker, sociologists should take the side of the 'underdogs,' or the oppressed. Table 7.1 summarizes Silverman's three research roles.

As an alternative to the question 'whose side are we on?' Silverman asks, who is our audience? He argues that the three roles listed above tend to ignore the more practical aspects of social research. For him, research is a social practice,

TABLE 7.2   *Audiences and their expectations*

Audience	Expectations
Academic Colleagues	Theoretical, factual or methodological insights
Policymakers	Practical information relevant to current policy issues
Practitioners	A theoretical framework for understanding clients better; factual information; practical suggestions for better procedures; reform of existing practices
The general public	New facts; ideas for reform of current practices or policies; guidelines for how to manage better or get better service from practitioners or institutions; assurances that others share their own experiences of particular problems in life

Source: Strauss and Corbin 1990: 242–43, as cited in Silverman 2001: 267

one that emerges in a particular social context for a particular purpose. Silverman returns our attention to the practical goals of research by underscoring how different types of research meet the needs of different audiences, such as academics, policymakers, practitioners, and the general public. Accordingly, as seen in Table 7.2, each audience has its own expectations about the value and utility of research and, therefore, makes different demands about what issues should be addressed by researchers.

CHAPTER SUMMARY

This chapter reviewed the ethics of social research as they apply to qualitative methods. These ethics can loosely be defined as the dos and don'ts of how we treat our research participants. A number of general principles were described. It was emphasized that we should ensure that participation is voluntary, no harm comes to the respondents, the research is of some benefit to the participants, and that their privacy will be protected. One way of addressing all these concerns is through the informed consent process whereby verbal or written statements are shared with research participants to inform them about the topic of the study, its potential benefit or harm, and the specific steps taken to guard their privacy. Some limitations of the informed consent guidelines were briefly discussed. In particular, I argued that in qualitative research it is difficult to fully describe the study to the respondents from the start, because the questions and themes emerge deductively over time. I concluded the chapter with Silverman's three research roles: the scholar, the state counselor, and the partisan, and suggested that as an alternative to asking 'whose side are we on?' researchers could consider the specific audience for whom they are writing.

SUGGESTED READINGS

A more thorough discussion of ethics in qualitative research can be found in Clifford G. Christians' chapter 'Ethics and Politics in Qualitative Research' in the second edition of the *Handbook of Qualitative Research* (2000). Similarly, Silverman's chapter 'Relevance and Ethics' in *Interpreting Qualitative Data* (2001) is both in-depth and theoretically astute. Finally, the American Sociological Association offers its own code of ethics, which is available online through their website (www.asanet.org).

EXERCISE 7.1

OBJECTIVE: To develop a standard research consent form based on the discussions from this chapter.

DESCRIPTION: Using the example provided in this chapter as a model, develop an informed consent form for a qualitative study of dating among teenagers. Include the following elements: 1. brief description of the project and its data collection methods (e.g., interviews); 2. potential harm and benefit to the respondents; and 3. safeguards for protecting the respondents' privacy.

EXERCISE 7.2

OBJECTIVE: To encourage students to reflect on the ethical problems they might encounter while conducting their own research.

DESCRIPTION: Write a short essay detailing the ethical problems raised by the Laud Humphreys' *Tearoom Trade*. In your view, what ethical principles did the researcher violate? Did the scientific benefits of the research outweigh the risk of harm to the participants? How could his topic be studied in a way that does not pose a risk to the research participants?

Glossary

Action-oriented research: research designed to produce concrete changes in the respondents' lives and their surrounding community.

Active interviewing: a type of unstructured approach to data collection that treats the interview as a social occasion for reality production.

Analysis: also referred to as findings or results, is the part of a paper that presents the data along with the researcher's interpretation.

Anonymity: The condition where not even the researcher knows the respondents' identities.

Autoethnography: a type of ethnography that uses the researcher's personal experiences and emotions as a source of data.

Conclusion: the final part of the research paper that summarizes the findings, discusses implications, and points to possibilities for further research.

Confidentiality: The safeguards taken by researchers to protect the identities of known respondents.

Constructionism: a philosophical orientation that focuses on how human practices create social reality.

Content analysis: the analysis of qualitative data using a systematic approach that involves sampling, coding and sometimes quantification.

Conversation analysis: the analysis of social interaction with the goal of understanding how reality is interactionally achieved through talk.

Data analysis: the interpretive work of conceptually connecting human artifacts with other meaningful information.

Data display: organizing and displaying the data in a way that facilitates interpretation and analysis.

Data reduction: the process of reducing data into more manageable and relevant segments.

Discourse: a way of understanding, knowing, and speaking that rhetorically and practically orients us toward the social world.

Ethnographic interview: a variant of unstructured interviews that is particularly sensitive to the social context of the respondents' lives.

Ethnography: a qualitative research approach based on observing, participating in, and recording a people's way of life or social experiences.

Field: the specific setting or place where ethnographic research is done.

Field role: the social position an ethnographer assumes or is assigned to in the field.

Focus group: interviewing a group of respondents at the same time with the goal of stimulating discussion.

Focused coding: organizing the data into more substantially and theoretically meaningful categories as part of grounded theory analysis.

Going native: the presumed problem of an ethnographer over-identifying or over-sympathizing with research subjects.

Hypotheses: educated guesses or hunches about the relationship between certain concepts or variables.

In-depth interview: a variant of unstructured interviews with special emphasis on revealing the respondents' inner feelings and attitudes.

Informant: an insider or a respondent who works closely with the researcher and becomes the ethnographer's guide, expert, or ally in the field.

Informed consent: A verbal or written description that informs respondents regarding the purpose of the research project and its potential benefits and harms.

Initial coding: organizing the data into general categories or themes before more in-depth codes are developed. This is typically a component of grounded theory analysis.

Institutional ethnography: ethnographic research that is explicitly about how human activities are shaped by institutional policies and practices.

Interview: collecting information by asking questions and receiving answers through face-to-face, phone, or internet interaction.

Introduction: the first part of a research paper that introduces the topic and the review of relevant scientific literature.

Methodology: a general orientation about how research is done.

Methods: specific research techniques for investigating a topic.

Narrative: a way of representing information based on a particular order (e.g., clear beginning, middle and end) and genre.

Narrative practice: the activities that make a story meaningful and coherent in order to meet the needs of a particular setting or occasion.

Natural attitude: a taken-for-granted view of the social world based on common sense.

Polling: surveying large groups of people to learn their opinions about a particular social issue or a commercial product.

Positivism: a theoretical model for conducting social research modeled after the natural sciences and based on a search for universal laws and strictly empirical evidence.

Postmodernism: an interdisciplinary movement that is based on the relentless critique of established social conventions.

Qualitative research: methodological techniques for analyzing the nuances or the quality of human experience.

Quantitative research: methodological techniques that represent the human experience in numerical or statistical forms.

Rapport: a sense of respect, trust and mutual obligation that aids the ethnographer in soliciting information from his respondents.

Reliability: the extent to which the research findings can be replicated over time and/or by other investigators.

Schedule: a list of questions that are asked verbatim, or word-for-word, from a respondent during a structured interview.

Scientific investigation: logically connecting certain systematic empirical facts or observations with an explanation of those facts.

Scientific rigor: systematic adherence to certain rules and procedures for conducting research.

Self-administered questionnaire: a list of questions that can be answered by the respondent without the presence of or assistance from the researcher.

Self-presentation: the process and practices through which we present ourselves to others and are perceived by them.

Semiotics: the study of signs, or the visual in general, both in relation to surface meaning and deeper cultural relevance.

Social desirability effect: the presumed tendency among respondents to disguise their 'true' attitudes by answering questions in a socially acceptable way.

Social science research: the act of reexamining the social world with the goal of better understanding or explaining why or how people behave.

Sociology: a social science that aims to empirically appreciate the complexity of human life.

Structured interview: an interviewing technique that relies on closed-ended questions and strict procedures for collecting data.

Talk: everyday conversations that are not solicited by researchers.

Text: recorded information about social life in the form of visual images, published material, or transcribed interviews.

Unstructured interview: an interviewing technique based on open-ended questions that encourage respondents to elaborate on their statements.

Validity: the extent to which the research findings or concepts correspond to empirical reality.

Visual culture: cultural literacy of, and everyday experience with, visual materials (photos, films, videos and so on).

Voluntary participation: The ethical principle that requires respondents not to be psychologically or physically forced to participate in research.

References

Adler, P. 1997. 'Researching Dealers and Smugglers.' pp. 55–70 in *Constructions of Deviance: Social Power, Context, and Interaction*, 2nd ed., edited by P. A. Adler and P. Adler. Belmont, CA: Wadsworth.

Adler, P. and P. Adler. 1987. *Membership Roles in Field Research.* Newbury Park, CA: Sage.

Anderson, E. 1997. 'The Police and the Black Male.' pp. 142–152 in *Constructions of Deviance: Social Power, Context, and Interaction*, 2nd ed., edited by P. A. Adler and P. Adler. Belmont, CA: Wadsworth.

Arocha, Z. 1980. Untitled, *The Miami Herald.* October 31, 1980, p. 3B.

Atkinson, P. 1992. *Understanding Ethnographic Texts.* Thousand Oaks, CA: Sage.

Atkinson, P. 1997. 'Narrative Turn of Blind Alley?' *Qualitative Health Research* 7(3): 325–344.

Atkinson, P. and D. Silverman. 1997. Kundera's Immorality: The Interview Society and the Invention of Self.' *Qualitative Inquiry* 3(3): 324–345.

Austin, J. L. 1962. *How To Do Things With Words.* Oxford: Clarendon.

Babbie, E. 2002. *The Basics of Social Research.* 2nd ed. Belmont, CA: Wadsworth.

Baker, C. 1997. 'Membership Categorization and Interview Accounts.' pp. 129–143 in *Qualitative Research: Method, Theory and Practice*, edited by D. Silverman. London: Sage.

Ball, M. and G. Smith. 1992. *Analyzing Visual Data.* Thousand Oaks, CA: Sage.

Ball, M. and G. Smith. 2001. 'Technologies of Realism? Ethnographic Uses of Photography and Film.' pp. 302–319 in *Handbook of Ethnography*, edited by P. Atkinson, A. Coffey, S. Delamont, J. Lofland and L. Lofland. London: Sage.

Bamberger, M. 1999. *Integrating Quantitative and Qualitative Research in Development Projects.* Washington D. C.: World Bank.

Barkan, S. E. and S. F. Cohn. 1994. 'Racial Prejudice and Support for the Death Penalty by Whites.' *Journal of Research in Crime and Delinquency* 31: 202–9.

Barthes, R. 1967. *Elements of Semiology.* London: Cape.

Baszanger, I. and N. Dodier. 1997. 'Ethnography: Relating the Part to the Whole.' pp. 8–23 in *Qualitative Research: Theory, Method and Practice*, edited by D. Silverman. London: Sage.

Bateson, G. and M. Mead. 1942. *The Balinese Character: A Photographic Analysis.* New York: New York Academy of Sciences.

Bauer, M. W. 2000. 'Classical Content Analysis: A Review.' pp. 131–151 in *Qualitative Researching with Text, Image and Sound.* London: Sage.

Becker, H. S. 1963. *Outsiders: Studies in the Sociology of Deviance.* New York: Free Press.

Becker, H. S. 1967. 'Whose Side Are We On?' *Social Problems* 14: 239–248.

Becker, H. S. 1974. 'Photography and Sociology'. *Studies in the Anthropology of Visual Communication* 1(1): 3–26.

Becker, H. S. 1975. 'Photography and Sociology.' *Afterimage* 3: 22–32.

Becker, H. S. 1981. *Exploring Society Photographically.* Chicago: University of Chicago Press.

Becker, H. S. 1993. 'Becoming a Marijuana User.' pp.185–196 in *Social Deviance: Readings in Theory and Research*, edited by H. Pontell. Englewood Cliffs, NJ: Prentice Hall.

Berg, B. L. 2001. *Qualitative Research Methods for the Social Sciences*, 4th ed. Boston: Allyn & Bacon.

Berger, L. 2001. 'Inside Out: Narrative Autoethnography as a path Toward Rapport.' *Qualitative Inquiry* 7(4): 504–518.

Best, S. and D. Kellner. 1991. *Postmodern Theory: Critical Interrogations*. New York: The Guilford Press.

Blackmar, F. W. 1897. 'The Smoky Pilgrims.' *American Journal of Sociology*, 2: 485–500.

Bloor, M., J. Frankland, M. Thomas and K. Robson. 2001. *Focus Groups in Social Research*. London: Sage.

Blumer, H. 1969. *Symbolic Interactionism: Perspective and Method*. Berkeley, CA: University of California Press.

Cajacob, C. 1980. Untitled letter to the editor. *The Miami Herald*. October 27, p. 6A.

Chaplin, E. 1994. *Visual Representation in Sociology*. London: Routledge.

Charmaz, K. 2002. 'Qualitative Interviewing and Grounded Theory Analysis.' pp. 675–694 in *Handbook of Interview Research: Context and Method*, edited by J. Gubrium and J. Holstein. Thousand Oaks, CA: Sage.

Chion, M. 1994. *Audio-Vision: Sound on Screen*. New York: Columbia University Press.

Christians, C. G. 2000. Ethics and Politics in Qualitative Research. pp. 133–155 in *Handbook of Qualitative Research*, 2nd ed., N.K. Denzin and Y. Lincoln Eds. Thousand Oaks, CA: Sage.

Clayman, S. C. 1992. 'Footing in Achievement of Neutrality: The Case of News Interview Discourse.' pp. 163–198 in *Talk at Work*, edited by P. Drew and J. C. Heritage. Cambridge: Cambridge University Press.

Coffey, A. and P. Atkinson. 1996. *Making Sense of Qualitative Data: Complementary Research Strategies*. London: Sage.

Cortazzi, M. 2001. 'Narrative Analysis in Ethnography.' pp. 384–394 in *Handbook of Ethnography*, edited by P. Atkinson, A. Coffey, S. Delamont, J. Lofland, and L. Lofland. London: Sage.

Creswell, J. W. 2003. *Research Design: Qualitative, Quantitative, and Mixed Methods Approaches*. Thousand Oaks, CA: Sage.

Cushing, F. H. 1979. *Zuni: Selected Writings of Frank Hamilton Cushing*. Lincoln, NB: University of Nebraska Press.

Deegan, M. J. 2001. 'The Chicago School of Ethnography.' pp. 11–25 in *Handbook of Ethnography*, edited by P. Atkinson, A. Coffey, S. Delamont, J. Lofland and L. Lofland. London: Sage.

Denzin, N. 1970. *The Research Act in Sociology*. London: Butterworth.

Denzin, N. 1991. *Images of Postmodern Society*. Newbury Park, CA: Sage.

Denzin, N. 1995. *The Cinematic Society: The Voyeur's Gaze*. Thousand Oaks, CA: Sage.

DeVault, M.L. and L. McCoy. 2002. 'Institutional Ethnography: Using Interviews to Investigate Ruling Relations.' pp. 751–776 in *Handbook of Interview Research: Context and Method*, edited by J. Gubrium and J. Holstein. Thousand Oaks, CA: Sage.

Douglas, J. D. 1985. *Creative Interviewing*. Beverly Hills, CA: Sage.

Dunbar, C., Jr., D. Rodriguez and L. Parker. 2002. 'Race, Subjectivity, and the Interview Process.' pp. 279–298 in *Handbook of Interview Research: Context and Method*, edited by J. Gubrium and J. Holstein. Thousand Oaks, CA: Sage.